IS HE MR. RIGHT?

ALSO BY MIRA KIRSHENBAUM

The Weekend Marriage:
Abundant Love in a Time-Starved World

Everything Happens for a Reason:
Finding the True Meaning of the Events in Our Lives

The Emotional Energy Factor:
The Secrets High-Energy People Use to Beat Emotional Fatigue

Too Good to Leave, Too Bad to Stay:
A Step-by-Step Guide to Help You Decide
Whether to Stay In or Get Out of Your Relationship

The Gift of a Year:
How to Give Yourself the Most Meaningful,
Pleasurable, and Satisfying Year of Your Life

Women & Love:
The Eight Make-or-Break Experiences of Love in Women's Lives

Our Love Is Too Good to Feel So Bad:
The 10 Prescriptions to Heal Your Relationship

Parent/Teen Breakthrough:
The Relationship Approach (with Dr. Charles Foster)

IS HE MR. RIGHT?

*Everything
You Need
to Know
Before
You Commit*

MIRA KIRSHENBAUM

Harmony Books / New York

Copyright © 2006 by Mira Kirshenbaum

Published in the United States by Harmony Books, an imprint of the Crown
Publishing Group, a division of Random House, Inc., New York.
www.crownpublishing.com

Harmony Books is a registered trademark and the Harmony Books colophon
is a trademark of Random House, Inc.

Library of Congress Cataloging-in-Publication Data

Kirshenbaum, Mira.
Is he Mr. Right? : everything you need to know before you commit / Mira
Kirshenbaum.—1st ed.
1. Mate selection.   2. Man-woman relationships.   I. Title.
HQ801.K566 2006
646.7'7—dc22   2005030885

ISBN-13: 978-0-307-33673-6
ISBN-10: 0-307-33673-5

Printed in the United States of America

Design by Chris Welch

10   9   8   7   6   5   4   3   2   1

First Edition

To Nicolas,
the new Mr. Right in my life

Acknowledgments

No question about it—I've never had more people to thank for any book I've ever written. And that means I'm incredibly lucky. That so many people would go so far to help me is amazing.

I'm talking first about all the women, and a lot of men, too, who participated in the research for this book. You know who you are. Your generosity and honesty were spectacular.

Some of you took the time to write detailed answers to a very long, open-ended questionnaire. Your answers poured in from all over the United States and from every part of the world. A woman from Warsaw wrote thirty pages, and I wouldn't have wanted to miss a single one.

Some of you, not quite so many, participated in telephone or in-person interviews. You were busy people, and yet you never gave me less than an hour. Two hours was common. And in that time you shared amazingly personal details in an amazingly thoughtful way.

And some of you were my patients. I'm honored that you came to me for help, and I'm grateful for your honesty and willingness to change and grow. Sometimes you were my laboratory, as you know, and yet you trusted me.

I thank you all from the bottom of my heart.

And I'm grateful for all the ways you came to me. Though

this was not a scientifically determined random sample, I know from the things you told me about yourselves that you represent the full spectrum of women and men in America today. Many of you came to me in a viral kind of way. You passed someone on to me who passed someone on to me who . . . The chains could get very long. Sometimes when I wanted to cast my net wider, I used communities like Craigslist or Soul Graffiti to generate volunteer responders. I want to thank everyone who made this possible. With Craigslist, there were times when I posted a request for responders and got flooded with volunteers immediately after the posting. It made me very happy.

Next I want to thank my partner, Dr. Charles Foster. He was responsible for most of the research, and he was my full partner, 50/50, in writing this book. This was a true and total collaboration—every word of it is as much his as it is mine. I can't thank him enough.

Speaking of the men in my life, I owe a huge debt of gratitude to my agent extraordinaire, Howard Morhaim. For more than ten years, Howard's experience and wisdom and generous heart have meant everything to me. It just keeps getting better.

There are a lot of wonderful people at Harmony that I need to thank.

From the moment I first laid eyes on her, Julia Pastore defined herself as someone with enormous integrity and intelligence. I feel very lucky to have Julia as my editor, and I hope we do many more books together. She's a pleasure to work with. Thanks also to Kathryn Kennedy for keeping things going and making sure everything works well.

I want to thank Kim Meisner for launching this project. She was there at the conception, and I'm very grateful to her for getting what I was trying to do and letting me run with the ball.

As always, many thanks and much affection to my generalissimo, Shaye Areheart, who's helped me and my work for over twenty years. Shaye, you really are the best.

Selina Cicogna and Kira Stevens have brought enormous energy and talent to publicity and marketing. You guys are great. And a big thanks too to Tara Gilbride for her contributions.

Many, many thanks to Dan Rembert and Laura Duffy for their beautiful, chic, and effective jacket. A home run!

Big thanks to Andrea Peabbles, who was not only a smart and careful copy editor, but who understood where I was coming from and enhanced the flavor of my work.

And finally, thanks to Jill Flaxman and all the other amazing people who've worked so hard on behalf of this book.

There are people on my team here at Chestnut Hill who I very much want to thank. There's Christine Harbaugh, my brilliant and sweet blog and Web designer and master. Thanks for the look and functionality of all my Web sites. And a deep thank-you to the people here who make my life function and enable me to get my work done without going nuts—Toby Desroches, Nikki Green, and Doc Miner.

Finally, a ton of gratitude and lots of hugs and kisses to Rachel and Hannah Kirshenbaum, Michael Motta, and Dan Bernunzio, who always come through for me and who came through big time for this book.

CONTENTS

ALL ABOUT YOU

ABOUT THE STAGE YOUR RELATIONSHIP IS IN

YOUR FINAL STEP

WHY I WROTE THIS BOOK,
AND WHY YOU SHOULD READ IT

Too many of us choose the wrong guys for the wrong reasons and then stay with them for too long. What a waste! I've felt for a long time that we can do much better. The seed for this book was planted the day Michelle came to see me. Her love life was driving her crazy. For two years she'd been with a guy she'd hoped was the love of her life. Sometimes he made her happy. But she'd finally accepted what she'd been denying for too long—he was too often angry, selfish, and negative.

"Mira," she said, "how the *hell* do you know if a guy is right for you? I'm so sick of wasting time in relationships that go nowhere." She sighed. "Why is all this so hard? In some ways he's great. But I don't want to be with him just to end up getting divorced. And I don't want to be alone. It feels scary for me to dump a guy just because I have my doubts."

There was something about Michelle—bright, warm, sweet, deserving all the best that life has to offer—that touched my heart. She went on, "Is there something wrong with me? My ability to trust guys is at a minimum now. I'm so ashamed to be in this situation. Shouldn't I know if he's the one?" She paused. "Maybe I should just suck it up and commit to him."

I'll spare you the gory details, but looking back, Michelle had pretty much chosen the wrong guys the same way we might choose the wrong melons. We thump, squeeze, sniff, but we don't know what to look for. I thought, Wow, if Michelle's history of choosing men is what normal gets you, what happens to those of us who are a little screwed up?

At one point I blurted out, "You've made every mistake in the book."

"What book?" Michelle joked.

"Well, I *wish* there were a book," I said.

"So you should write it," Michelle said. I told her I'd try my best.

For years I'd dreamed of a crystal ball for sizing up guys. As a therapist I've seen thousands of women who have wasted time with guys they never should've committed to in the first place. It breaks my heart. And these women are just a small sampling of the millions of women in the same boat. Twenty percent of first marriages drop dead in the first five years. This is just the tip of the iceberg of the many people getting together who don't belong together. It's nuts! Why can't we identify the guy who's right for us in the first place?

So I rolled up my sleeves and set about figuring out what's most important when you're choosing someone to share your life. With the help of my partner, Dr. Charles Foster, I interviewed women who were happy with their decision to commit and those who regretted it, women from Los Angeles to New York, Seattle to Atlanta, Amsterdam to Tokyo. White, Black, Asian, Latina. Rural, urban, suburban. Gay and straight. Rich and poor. PhD's from Harvard and PhD's from the School of Hard Knocks. I heard all their war stories, all the anger and humor and pain at what they'd gone through trying to figure out if some guy was right for them. I interviewed a lot of men, too.

All that has brought forth *Is He Mr. Right?* This book is the crystal ball I'd dreamed of. It will give you everything you need to see if *your* guy is Mr. Right, and not Mr. Wrong, not Mr.

Right-Now, not Mr. Oh-My-God-What-Demented-State-Was-I-in-to-Get-Involved-with-This-Jerk.

At the heart of this book is a brand-new understanding of the one most important factor that determines whether a guy is right for you—chemistry, and this is the first book that shows you exactly what chemistry is and how to know if you have it. You'll discover the secret of women who end up finding love. You'll see how to distinguish the real thing from the counterfeit. You'll understand why you've gone in and out of relationships that weren't satisfying. You'll be able to tell the difference between guys who are keepers and those who are losers. You'll know the signs that show whether you can trust a guy or not. You'll learn to prevent your own issues from blinding you to who's right for you. You'll see what to pay attention to at every stage. By the end, you'll know *everything* you need to know before you go any further in your relationship.

Finally, you'll get the clarity you've been hungry for. Of course the final decision is up to you, but I'll make no bones about telling you, "Dump this guy!" if that's what the signs point to. I'll show you plenty of good signs too, because there are a lot of good guys out there. Maybe you've found one already!

ESSENTIALS

LOOKING INTO YOUR FUTURE

A t any point between your first date and your wedding night, your heart can be gripped by the question, *Is this guy my dreamboat or my* Titanic? *The man I was always meant to be with or a big fat waste of time? A keeper or a loser?*

Wouldn't it be great if you could look into a crystal ball and know, like, *today*, "Will this guy make me happy? Is this love that will last? Or, if I keep going forward with him, am I just settling? Is there someone else out there who's even better for me—I wouldn't want to miss out on the love of my life! Or is this guy Mr. Right?"

There are two possibilities:

1. He might have great qualities and love you, but *he's just not the one*. He won't make you happy. If you commit to him, things will turn out badly. So you've got to say goodbye, shed some tears, and move on to someone better.

2. Even if your guy is a gap-toothed goofball, he's *your* gap-toothed goofball. Somehow his being the way he is and your being the way you are feels right and works well. He will make you happy. And if you commit, you will have a great future together. So—you've got to move forward with him.

But which is true for you?
Figuring this out can easily make the smartest woman feel stupid. Your guy, of course, is a mixed bag. As far as you can tell, he's not Mr. Right or Mr. Wrong. He's Mr. Maybe. They say you can't compare apples and oranges—well, he's Carmen Miranda's whole hat, and how do you add up a hatful of different fruit?

Kelly, 31, said, "Okay, let's see. In favor of his being Mr. Right is the fact that we both like barbecues, baseball, and big dogs. We both hate to get up in the morning or go to sleep at night. We both went to John F. Kennedy Middle School, although in different cities! In favor of his being Mr. Wrong is the fact that we fight a lot over stupid things. I want three kids; he's not sure he wants one. We rarely want to make love at the same time. We get on each other's nerves when we're both in the kitchen."

Sigh. . . . If only relationships weren't so confusing. And the early stages are the *most* confusing. Fears are churning. Hopes are peeping through like crocuses through the snow. Worst of all, solid information is hard to get. When friends ask how we feel about him, we respond with a stir-fry of contradictory feelings. All we know is that we're searching for certainty, but we're not sure how to find it. There's so little to go on. He seems nice, but is he really Hannibal Lecter in sheep's clothing? He seems distant—is he cold or is he just shy?

Even when you do grab hold of a clue, it can be hard to know what it means. Let's say you're a real beach bunny. Then you discover that your guy hates the beach. What do you do? Your friends have opinions ("But he makes so much money!" "But you live for the beach!"). Will he come around? you wonder. Will you get tired of the beach? (*Never!*) Will you find a way to work around this? Will it drive a wedge between you?

The Fork in the Road

Almost any woman in a developing relationship is hungry for certainty these days. Take Laura, 33. She'd been sitting next to me while we were waiting to board a plane. They'd announced a delay. Since we were going to be there for God knows how long, we started chatting.

She said she was at that stage where it was starting to feel like she and her boyfriend, Jack, should talk about making some kind of commitment. Maybe to move in together. "But I'm afraid Jack isn't right for me," Laura said with a queasy look I've seen thousands of times, a look you see on the faces of first-time skydivers. "We've gone out for five months and had lots of those phone calls where you talk for hours about everything and nothing. That's the good part."

Laura leaned toward me. "But I'm not nuts about Jack. I care about him, but shouldn't I be feeling I'm crazy about him at this point? Something's missing—I just don't know what. Magic or something. But what am I, a teenager? Do you need magic and bells and birds singing? I'm afraid I have unrealistic expectations. He's good. We're good together. *He got me a promise ring.*" Laura was silent for a minute. "But what if this is something I'm just telling myself because, let's face it, I want to get married? I'm at a real fork in the road. If Jack and I aren't right for each other, I'd get out now if I were smart. Right?

"Wouldn't it be great if there were a way to just not care about the guy until he was totally in love with you and you'd totally checked him out? But women don't work that way, do we? We put our heart on the line and . . . I don't know—the whole thing makes you so vulnerable and I hate that. I mean, I really like falling in love, but I don't like the feeling that the whole thing is so iffy."

THE SEARCH FOR CERTAINTY

Developing relationships are confusing, but we do our best. It gets frustrating when the things we do to gain certainty only make us more confused.

We've tried asking ourselves, "Do I love him?" After all, shouldn't you just know? And if you do know, shouldn't it make a difference? But after you roll this around in your head for a while . . . it's so complicated. Sure, you love him, but the more you think about it, the less clear you are about what the word *love* even means. That you're hot for him? That you have "feelings" for him? That you think about him a lot? That you miss the good things about him when he's not around? (And what good does that do, if when he is around he drives you crazy?)

Let's face it, thinking about love can be a very confusing way to figure out if he's Mr. Right. Just think about some of the losers you've loved in the past.

Another thing we've tried is endlessly analyzing every detail about him and about the relationship. What's up with his staring at you the way he does when you kiss or make love? What's that whistling sound in his left nostril, and will it make you want to kill him one day? Why is it that every time the two of you get really close you end up having a fight?

It's like trying to read tea leaves, but so far all you've gotten is a soggy mess of confusion.

THE GUY SPEAKS: *"I hate it when a woman goes on and on analyzing every detail of our relationship. It's so discouraging, and honestly it makes me feel she doesn't like me. I just keep feeling, if we were happy together, if we were meant to be, would we need to do all this overanalyzing?"**

*From time to time you'll get comments from the guy's point of view. These are taken from what the men I interviewed told me.

We've also tried endlessly analyzing our own motives. *Why* do you want to be with him? Is it low self-esteem? Pressure from family and friends? Fear you can't do better? The problem is that if you lift up the top of your head, you find a whole *jungle* of motives in there, and how do you sort them out?

And of course we've tried searching for compatibility. You know, if you like dogs, it would be nice to be with someone who also likes dogs. The problem is that there may have been plenty of times when you found a guy who shared your values and tastes and yet you just didn't connect at all. As it turns out, compatibility isn't really much to go on when it comes to seeing if someone's your Mr. Right.

What this adds up to is that you've been searching, searching, searching for a sign, like a safecracker turning the combination lock, turning, turning, hoping that suddenly the tumblers will fall into place and *pop*, the door will open. Maybe you'll have that one perfect day with your guy that answers all your questions. Maybe you'll have that one awful fight that shows you what a snake he really is. But you haven't found that sign yet. And now you're starting to wonder if it's ever going to show up. It's scary. What if you drift forever, never knowing?

And so you get stuck in ambivalence. Limbo. You drift. Maybe, you wonder, if you just stop thinking, just go with the flow, clarity will come to you. But of course clarity doesn't come this way. Drifting is what comes from drifting. It's like a narcotic—it's hard to break the habit.

The truth is that wasting time up in the air feels miserable. It drains your energy and your emotions. And it can lead to trouble. You can drift into a committed relationship you never really wanted. You can drift out of a relationship with a guy you'll later realize was Mr. Right.

But what if we've been going about this all wrong? Sure, your guy is a mixed bag, but what if we've been looking at the wrong things in trying to figure out if he is Mr. Right? That would be huge. It would explain why we've been so stuck in the search for certainty.

What if there were a way to look at your guy right now that will show you what your future together will look like? *There is.* Stay tuned.

Oops, Wrong Guy

Certainty is something we desperately need. The fact that we often don't know what's important to look at before we commit can cause us a lot of problems in our lives. Let me get personal. It caused me a lot of problems in my life.

My mother's great, but she had the same trouble knowing who was right for her that most of us have. My mother was a farm girl. When she met the man who would become my father, she thought he was very cool. Tall, handsome, romantic, artistic, and from a good family, he was also a rebel without a cause.

But were they right for each other? Tragically, all they had in common was that they both belonged to the same species. He was a trophy husband for her. For him, she was someone he thought he could dominate (boy, was he wrong!). Result? They got divorced when I was four and I didn't see him again until I was sixteen. My mother's little *oops, wrong guy* meant I never had a father.

My mother made another mistake when she got involved with my stepfather. By this time, she was a single mom working in a dress factory. She wasn't interested in handsome, artistic rebels anymore—she just wanted a guy who could take care of her and her kids.

Now picture the scene. I'm five and a half, playing on the streets of the Lower East Side of Manhattan, and I want a father like all the other kids. Down the street comes this guy wearing a Panama hat, a light tan suit, and brown-and-white shoes, making him the best-dressed man I'd ever seen.

I rolled into action. Acting all cute and everything, I charmed him and made him go and talk to my mother. I was basically pimping my mother to him, and I guess because I'd gotten him in a good mood he was very nice to her. He showed off, the way guys do, because my mom was pretty, and he made it seem as if he was more successful than he really was. So she glommed on to him. A few weeks later they stunned me by telling me they'd gotten married.

Again my mother had done what millions of us do—gotten involved with a guy because he had one good thing going for him, the very thing her previous guy lacked. I don't know if she ever asked herself how it felt to be with him. In fact, they got along horribly. The result was that basically my life from then on was all about hearing them scream at each other.

Now you can see one of the reasons I care so much. Why should you put yourself and your future children through what my mother and I went through?

IF YOU'RE WILLING TO SEE THE TRUTH

If you're looking for real love, I can help. And I'm sure real love *is* what you want. So okay—no more stupid mistakes, no more wasted time, no more heartache. All you need is to be willing to see the truth and to act on it.

THE GUY SPEAKS: *"I have to say I totally agree—love matters to me, too, and I want to get it right, too. Yeah, when I was younger I was happy to just screw around. But then suddenly you're in your thirties and you start thinking about having a family and guys you know have already gotten divorced. The one thing I want right now is to be in a relationship with someone where we're both right for each other. Where it feels right, so you just know it."*

I'm going to show you if your guy is Mr. Right. If you do your part, you'll never again get stuck in a dead-end relationship. I'll show you how to look into the future with him. You'll know if difficulties you've been having are meaningful. You'll know if the good things you have together are enough. You'll know if you have that magic glue that keeps love alive. You'll feel certain, and you'll be right.

If it turns out that he isn't Mr. Right, at least you'll know it, and you'll be freed up to find real love with a better guy. But if he is Mr. Right, your search and your suspense will be over. You'll be free to enjoy the love you've found.

The Secret to Knowing
If He's Mr. Right

So how do you know if your guy is right for you? I've spent most of my life looking for the answer to that question, and I'm sure you have too. I've rounded up all the usual suspects—love, compatibility, a consensus among your girlfriends, you name it—and I've tried to discover, *If this is what you have starting out, do you end up with a happy, healthy, long-lasting relationship that brings out the best in you?*

After getting input from more women than on any research project I've ever been involved with, I now see that the true answer is something very different from what I'd thought. The true answer is something that has the power to change all of our lives, save us endless heartache, and bring us a ton of happiness.

The best way to figure out if someone's right for you is to look at your chemistry. If real estate's all about location, location, location, relationships are all about chemistry, chemistry, chemistry.

My clinical experience confirms that when a couple doesn't have good chemistry, well, you just wouldn't want to bet money that their relationship will last. When they do have good chemistry, they usually end up having a good, long-lasting relationship.

So if you want to know if he's Mr. Right and if you'll be happy together, check out your chemistry.

HOW TO CHECK OUT YOUR CHEMISTRY

As you'll soon see, there are five dimensions to chemistry, and you need all five. But at heart, chemistry is all about how it feels to be together. All that really matters is how it feels when you're with each other.

> **Chemistry is not about compatibility, or how well you fit together. It's about how the fit you have feels to you. You have good chemistry if it feels good to be together. If it feels bad to be together, you have bad chemistry. If it feels like nothing much when you're together, you have no chemistry. That's it.**

You might be thinking that I'm talking about sexual chemistry. Well, that's a part of it, but there's a lot more to chemistry than that. You have good chemistry when it feels good going for a drive together. When it feels good just lying in bed and talking. When it feels good sharing problems with each other. When it feels good goofing off together. When it feels good the way you work things out after you get angry. When it feels good just knowing that you're in a relationship with each other.

Here's how people I talked to described having good chemistry:

- "I just feel at home with him. Like he's family, like I've known him my whole life. Plus we have so much fun together."
- "I think that on paper people wouldn't think we're all that suited for each other, but we just enjoy being with each other so much, even when things get stressful."

* "I feel we belong together. We just click. There's so much respect. And when we talk to each other there's a kind of happy flow."
* "We both have tempers, but even if we get mad at each other, it doesn't feel scary and it goes away very quickly. Then we'll start making out!"
* "My other relationships were a lot of work. We have some issues, but mostly it's trouble free. Mostly, I feel really safe with him."
* "When we're with each other, we can't keep our hands off each other, but it's funny because it's also so relaxed and easy."
* "There's this amazing connection between us. It's like he's my lover and my puppy and my best friend all at the same time."

Even if you always hated science in school—this is the kind of chemistry you gotta love. It's the kind that makes it clear that the two of you are right for each other.

CHEMISTRY STARTS AT THE BEGINNING

From the moment we lay eyes on a guy, we try to figure out the chemistry. I'm sure you've been on a first date and sat in a restaurant chatting back and forth across the table, and part of you seemed to kind of float out of your body and ask, "How does this really feel?" And some sort of reading came bubbling up.

Maybe you realized you felt bored or depressed. Bad chemistry. That tiny little joke you made hit the floor like a meatball—uh-oh, he doesn't get you. When he tried to impress you, he made you feel sorry for him instead. When he said something that should've made you feel sorry for him, you thought he was irritating. The supposedly clever things he said seemed horribly lame.

But maybe with the next guy you had that glimmer (or maybe a bonfire!) of feeling that *whoa!* maybe there's chemistry here. This one was getting under your skin—you felt intrigued, excited, connected, alive. He teased you, and it turned you on—how did he know to do that? Your little joke brought out a little joke from him, and the next thing you knew you were making each other laugh. Later when he told you his sister had died of cancer when they were both kids, he said it so simply you couldn't help feeling sad, and yet it made you strangely happy that things had happened to him that made him human.

Your feelings might not have been 100 percent positive, but they point to good chemistry. You found you were willing, maybe eager, to go along for the ride. At least as far as the next stop.

If there's good chemistry when you're first getting to know each other, you should trust it as a sign that it's worth moving forward.

In fact, chemistry is the most reliable indicator of whether or not you should move forward at every stage of your developing relationship.

THE GUY SPEAKS: *"I absolutely agree. Every time I've gotten stuck in a bad relationship it's because I didn't force myself to think about how it really felt for us to be together. Then one time instead of nitpicking the relationship to death a woman said to me, 'You know, we just don't do it for each other.' I was relieved. And when I finally did find good chemistry with a woman—well, it was clear. That's what I'd always been looking for."*

Not the Fit, but the Feel of the Fit

You can't predict chemistry. Many of us have set up friends we were 100 percent sure would get along great with each other, and yet when they met, they got on each other's nerves. And we've all had the experience of meeting the most unlikely person and right off things just click like mad.

Chemistry is the feel of your fit. So it should be natural to know if you have it or not. You just feel it. But of course we're human beings and we always find ways to complicate the most natural of things.

Take Nicole, 36. I asked her how she'd gotten involved with Sam.

"Honestly? I hate to admit this," she said in a quiet voice, "but I'd been going through a dry spell and of course I had Harry, who was six at the time. I was just happy to be going with someone. The big selling point with Sam was that we had very, very similar opinions about the environment and politics. The first time I went over to his house I noticed that he had four different recycling bins and I was like, 'Oh my God, I have four recycling bins, too.'

"So it was great that he was like me. 'Specially since Harry's dad and me were oil and water. The mistake I made was confusing *I'm like him* with *I like him*. It's so weird because you'd think you'd know it if you didn't click with someone. But I just didn't add it up. I mean, come on—you're having sex and agreeing about stuff, and so you try to ignore the fact that he's opinionated, he doesn't want to listen unless you're telling him how great he is, he says *uh* all the time, and each *uh* takes forever and you just have to sit there waiting for the genius to finish his, *uhhhhh*, thoughts—no, I didn't like him at all. But I didn't even see that when I thought I was starting to fall in love with him, because I totally confused compatibility and gratitude and a warm man in my bed with love."

Nicole had fallen for the belief that compatibility shows you who's Mr. Right. It's time we put compatibility in its place.

Compatibility is the idea that if, for example, you love golf and hate people who are late, you'll be happy with a guy if he also loves golf and also hates people who are late. The question is, does compatibility mean he's Mr. Right?

No! Compatibility has been way, way oversold. It's not the Holy Grail; it's really a red herring.

There are a lot of problems with using compatibility as a way of seeing if a guy is right for you. For one thing, it's very confusing. You both believe in staying in shape, but one of you likes tennis and the other likes hiking. You both like to go to bed early, but only one of you likes to sleep with the windows open. You both like sex, but one of you likes it kinky and the other likes it plain vanilla. How do you decide if you're compatible? You don't. *You can't.* It's too much of a hodgepodge.

For another thing, couples always get accustomed very quickly to the ways they're compatible. The fact that you've finally found someone who likes French food and Chinese movies instead of the other way around is nice at first but very soon it's no big deal. But the ways you're not compatible often become irritating. And that's what you're left with when the thrill from the ways you are compatible has left you. It's only having good chemistry that keeps the warm, loving, exciting feelings alive.

Most important, the fact that you may or may not be compatible doesn't really tell you what you want to know. Here's the truth.

Compatibility is a poor predictor of which couples will get divorced and which couples will be happy together.

There's plenty of research supporting the idea that people who are compatible on paper are no more likely than two people chosen at random to have what it takes to have a good relationship. Being compatible with someone has nothing to do with whether he's right for you.

I remember Jo, 27, who said, "Ninety percent of our relationship is good." Sounds great, doesn't it? But she was troubled. The 90 percent that was good was mostly on-paper-type things. Voting for the same candidates. Both liking wine and, oh boy, liking the *same* wines. Liking early hip-hop and late Beatles. Liking anchovies on pizza and the same stupid reality shows. The only teeny-weeny problem with this vision of near perfection was that *it didn't feel all that good to actually spend time together.* And that's what she called the 10 percent that wasn't so good.

If you're trying to meet guys, hey, looking for someone who shares your interests and attitudes is a good way to go. Some online sites are great for that. But you have to use them correctly. They're not going to tell you who's right for you. They're just going to offer candidates who are good on paper. But if you're trying to see if your guy is right for you, then it's chemistry, not compatibility, that tells you if he's Mr. Right.

Where Does Chemistry Come From?

If you want to ask me a really hard question, ask me where chemistry comes from. That's tough, but I'll tell you what I know. I know that if you have chemistry, you have it and it isn't going anywhere. Asking where it comes from is like asking where the cement in the foundation of your house comes from. Who knows, but that's not going anywhere, either.

And here's where I believe chemistry comes from. There's something about our deepest psychological natures that's oriented toward growing into greater strength and health and happiness. At our very core, we want to become our best selves. When you have chemistry, I believe it's because you've found a guy whose growth path meshes profoundly with yours. It's as if you've found the perfect partner for your journey in life.

And maybe this is just me, but I also believe there's a definite spiritual component to finding someone you have good chemistry with. It's as if God wants it to feel right when we've found the person who's right for us.

So it's too bad that we so often misread the chemistry.

GETTING CLEAR ABOUT YOUR CHEMISTRY

I've talked about how we confuse compatibility with chemistry. We also confuse lust with chemistry, gratitude with chemistry, thank-God-I'm-in-a-relationship with chemistry, being with a guy we can brag about with chemistry, finding a guy who has the one thing we need in the moment with chemistry. . . . And all of this can blind us to the fact that it just doesn't feel all that good to be with him.

Then there's the way the dating game itself distorts the process of reading your chemistry. Take the cliché—and I'm sure you and I have never done this!—where on the first couple of dates the woman pretends to be much nicer and sweeter than she really is ("You attract more flies with honey . . .") and the guy pretends to be more charming and together than he really is. They could have great but *totally phony* chemistry. The illusion of chemistry. Obviously, the chemistry between you and your guy can only be real if the two of you are being real.

You also can't be sure about your chemistry until you get used to each other and see each other in the real-life conditions of your day-to-day existence. When you're exhausted and irritable from work. When you're too tired to make an effort to fix yourselves up. When you get stuck in a routine. When you've run out of ways to impress each other. That's when you can see your true chemistry.

Chemistry's at the heart of the story I'm about to tell you. Once you hear it, you'll understand why you've had problems with relationships in the past. Now, for the first time, you'll be in a position to understand what chemistry is all about, what its dimensions are, how to read it, and also how we get into trouble and end up misreading it. And once you know how to read your chemistry, you'll know whether you should move forward with your guy.

Bottom line

You want a great relationship? The only thing you need to look at is your chemistry—how it feels when the two of you are together. If your chemistry's bad or there's little chemistry, your relationship won't be good no matter what else it has going for it. If your chemistry's great, he's Mr. Right.

Do You Have All
Five Dimensions of Chemistry?

"He was my first boyfriend in college," Jennifer, 28, said. "Actually he started out as my roommate's boyfriend. I hated my roommate and I figured I'd of course hate her boyfriend. Which I did kind of because he seemed like this lame hick. He liked this awful music. . . .

"But then they broke up—they didn't think it was any big deal—and I ran into him one day and we started talking. I don't know what it was—but it was like we just felt good together. Who'd have thunk it? Almost the minute we started talking it was like we could tell each other anything. I don't know which was more amazing—how vulnerable I was with him or how sweet and funny he seemed to me. And the big thing was that the more we got to know each other, the better it felt. Physically, emotionally, spiritually, you name it.

"Of course I screwed that relationship up completely because I was so young and stupid. When we got near graduation I kept saying I needed more time before I could make a commitment. I couldn't get over his being a hick. He just got sick of me putting him on hold. I don't know. All I know is that we were right for each other for no damn good reason at all except that it felt so right to be together in so many ways. He's the one that got away."

What was Jennifer getting at when she said, "it felt so right to be together in so many ways"?

THE FIVE DIMENSIONS

Jennifer was getting at the idea that chemistry is multi-dimensional. Chemistry is a specific feeling, but it's made up of different dimensions, like a salad. Just the way your favorite salad is made up of different flavors—sweet, tart, sour, bitter, salty—you can think of good chemistry as being made up of the different flavors of the two of you being together.

The research I did specifically for this book, plus all my years studying couples, shows me that good chemistry is, in fact, made up of five dimensions.

> **All five dimensions must be present for a guy to be your Mr. Right. When you have all five going, that's what I mean by good chemistry. Everything clicks. Chemistry is pass/fail. You have it or you don't. If one dimension is missing, he's not the one.**

Here are the five dimensions and specific ways to see whether each dimension is actually present in your relationship.

Dimension 1: You feel comfortable with each other and it's easy to get close.

> **In the long run, the most important dimension of chemistry is the sense of ease, peace, comfort, connection, and belonging.**

I'm talking about a sense of feeling at home with each other. This is the way people feel with their best friends—relaxed, comfortable, close, connected, and at ease. Words flow fully and easily.

"Are We Compatible?" quizzes just can't predict this. I know we're used to the idea that the more things you have in common with someone, the easier it is to be comfortable with him or her. Well sure, as long as you're talking superficial cocktail-party chitchat. But ultimately, you can't predict who you're going to have this kind of ease with. We fail to have it with people we should have it with. And we find we have it in spades with the most surprising people. But if you focus on how it really feels to you when you're with your guy, you won't go wrong.

Here's how to tell if you have this dimension of chemistry.

The signs. When you've got this dimension going for you, you genuinely like your guy and he makes you feel he likes you. It's easy to talk to and to listen to each other. Communication is open and it flows. You don't get bogged down. No eggshells. No walls. No barbed wire. No feeling judged. You feel you can easily get close, sharing your deepest thoughts and feelings in a way you don't with anyone else, and when you're close, it feels really good.

When might you specially test for this? While going for a long drive, or spending an evening together after a tough day at work, or sitting in a restaurant together. Any time it's just the two of you. If you've got this dimension of chemistry, at times such as these you have the sense that you're not being scrutinized, but are being accepted. You feel that you can be yourself. You can talk about whatever you like to talk about and know that good things will come of it. If you want to be quiet, that's fine, too.

Is this what you have with your guy? If not, there's no chemistry.

People get fooled about this because feeling comfortable doesn't have the excitement you might think comes with chemistry—as if chemistry meant there were lightning bolts shooting out of your fingertips. And it's certainly bad chemistry if you're bored with each other. But chemistry really means that the way you fit together feels good. It's like the way a perfect

French fry with the perfect amount of salt or ketchup feels in your mouth. Not exciting. Just right.

Feeling at ease is particularly important when you live through stressful situations together, such as moving to a new apartment or introducing him to your family. If you marry each other, you're going to live through a lot of stressful situations, and if the feeling of ease disappears the minute stress rears its ugly head, that's a bad sign.

But there's more. Being able to feel close and deeply connected to your guy is another essential part of this dimension.

The signs. It should feel easy to get as close as you want, and when you're close it should feel good. You can tell each other anything, all the things you've never told anyone else. You can share your darkest emotions and your wackiest thoughts. When you've been apart, it's not difficult to get close again. And the closer you get, the better it feels.

It's not that you'll always feel close. Busy times can make that impossible. But you always find you can get close without too much difficulty.

I don't want to be utopian. Most women in even the best relationships report feeling lonely every once in a while. But if you feel lonely with your guy "too often" or "most of the time," then that's a bad sign.

If you're not feeling close, feeling at ease is a sham, like putting wallpaper on a crumbling wall—it can't last long, and it sure isn't real.

Closeness is another word for "emotional intimacy," the kind that comes from showing who you really are as a person. And then feeling loved and cherished and accepted when you do so. And being able to love and cherish your partner when he does so. This may not always happen, of course, because sometimes we can't help smacking painfully into our partner's dark places. But generally you should feel that closeness and a sense of connection are as easy to get at as the food in your refrigerator. And as unlikely to make you sick.

But if you have to hide who you really are, it's not closeness. Then he's just a fellow passenger on a long-distance bus trip, someone you have to be polite to, otherwise you'll be at each other's throats.

> **If there's something that's making it hard to get close, or if you just don't feel a connection, you should trust that feeling. It's a bad sign. Don't go forward in this relationship as long as you're feeling that it's hard to get close.**

To sum up this dimension, you can't say you have chemistry unless you can say, "It feels comfortable for us to be together, it's easy to get close, and it feels really good when we do get close." *Is this what you have with your guy? If not, there's no chemistry.*

Dimension 2: You feel safe being in a relationship with him.

Is it too dramatic to talk about the need to feel safe in our relationships? After all, women today are used to taking care of ourselves. We're tougher than women have ever been at any other time in history. But safety doesn't just refer to knowing you won't be beaten or robbed, although that's certainly important. Safety reaches into the whole emotional realm.

The signs. Feeling safe with a guy means feeling you can breathe around him. Feeling you won't be lied to. Feeling that this guy doesn't have to have all the power, or control all the money. It means knowing he's not a guy who has "anger issues" or who can't forgive small mistakes, knowing he's not going to try to control you. You never experience him as being intentionally cruel. Arguing with him doesn't make you anxious.

Feeling safe means that the things he says and does rarely

hurt you and never scare you. You trust each other. You know where you stand. You don't have to hide who you are. In fact, you can show who you really are and feel accepted with all your flaws.

Safety also means security. It means your guy can take care of himself, hold down a job, earn a good living, pay his bills. If a neighbor's a bully, he can stand up to him. If his mother doesn't like you, he can stand up to her.

Safety means your guy isn't busy wrestling inner demons of depression, anxiety, or drug or alcohol dependency. These may have played a role in his past, but he has them under control now.

Safety also means your guy isn't eating himself into an early heart attack.

Safety means you can be honest, and when you're honest, it feels okay.

And safety means that whenever you're being you, the roof doesn't cave in.

Is this what you have with your guy? If not, there's no real, last-ing chemistry.

> THE GUY SPEAKS: *"You see, if she doesn't feel safe, I don't feel safe. Every time I've been in a relationship with a woman who didn't feel safe, whether it was my fault or not, and frankly sometimes it was my fault, our dynamic got so weird and uncomfortable. When women don't feel safe they get so angry or withdrawn or whatever. The whole thing is a horror show."*

Let's put this in perspective. Safety doesn't mean he's your daddy. I hope you both expect each other to stand on your own two feet and be responsible for your own lives. And safety does not mean that he's perfect. It's fine if he's filled with the nor-mal flaws most of us are filled with. Sometimes he'll drop the ball. Sometimes he'll step on your toes. Sometimes his needs will clash with your needs. Sometimes you'll have to pick up the slack.

And sometimes he'll get angry with you. You're actually safer if he expresses his anger. I'm not talking about calling you names, punching holes in walls, or anything else that scares or humiliates you. I'm talking about his genuinely expressing real feelings. The reason this makes you safer is that the information that comes out lets you know where you stand. Your guy won't go along with something you do that he really doesn't like and then one day completely blow up or get back at you or just dump you.

If too often you feel tense, fearful, scrutinized, unable to be yourself with him, then the dimension of safety is missing. You haven't yet found your Mr. Right.

Dimension 3: You feel it's fun to be together.
No, it doesn't have to be a constant laugh riot, although that might be nice. I just mean fun as opposed to grim.

You never know who you're going to have fun with. I play tennis. I can't tell you how many times somebody said, "Oh, you've got to play with so-and-so. You guys have so much in common." And I'd find myself playing tennis with a woman (check) who was a therapist (check) and was Jewish (check) and who'd maybe even grown up in New York (check), et cetera, et cetera, but it would be no fun at all. When it comes to fun, compatibility isn't all it's cracked up to be.

Then one day I happened to start talking to this woman who was waiting for a court. We hit it off, and for some weird reason we have all the fun in the world playing bad tennis together. This woman and I come from completely different backgrounds, never like the same movies, and I'll bet we'd find we disagree about politics, but for some reason out on the courts we run around like crazy and laugh until our bellies hurt.

The signs. It's easy to have fun with him and you have a lot of it. And that pleasurable feeling isn't wiped out by the routine and stress of everyday life.

Fun is the glue of intimacy. There's got to be a lightness, laughter, play, maybe silliness when you're together. Not all the time, of course. Maybe not even most of the time. But you have to know it's there for you. It can't feel far away like an impossible dream or a memory you can't recapture.

> THE GUY SPEAKS: *"Some women I've been with just didn't get how important fun is to a relationship. I think it sort of makes it all come together. You relax, you get close, everything feels right. Fun is one of the first things I look for that tells me maybe we belong together."*

And of course it's up to you what fun is. It could be talking politics. Or that could be your worst nightmare. It could be playing Scrabble. Or not, ever. Preparing food together. Or just eating food together. It may have nothing to do with what you do, just the way you do it. Some couples have more fun shopping for a car than others do at a pool party.

It doesn't count if you have fun together only because you do fun things together. If you need barbecues and roller coasters to have fun, then you don't have fun as part of your chemistry. Fun has to be there when it's just the two of you and no props.

Is this what you have with your guy? If not, there's no chemistry.

Is this raising the bar too high? I wondered about that myself. But among all the couples I've known, couples who were never able to have much fun with each other were much more likely to have unhappy relationships and to get divorced. Couples who do have this dimension of chemistry going for them have a shortcut to intimacy and a buffer against the stressful times we all face.

Whatever your idea of fun, you can't say you really
have chemistry unless you can say, "We have fun together."

Dimension 4: You have real affection and passion for each other.

This is where sexual chemistry comes in. And don't think you
get a free ride just because you're young and horny. Almost any
two young, horny people can get something going. Sexual
chemistry means more than this. It means there's something
you recognize as special about the way you're together physically, and about the way you want to be together.

It can be tricky to get a good read on this dimension. When
you're first getting to know each other, you may not have much
to go on. Then part of it can be confused by the fact that you're
driven by lust. And it can take a while to see if you have the
kind of sexual chemistry that lasts past the point where you've
gotten used to each other.

But you've got to check it out, because while no dimension
of chemistry is more important than any other, sexual chemistry
is the one dimension that's unique to your being a romantic
couple.

The signs. You feel there's a lot of affection back and forth,
verbal, emotional, physical. And it's the kind of affection you see
with people who are lovers. And the things you do to show affection and passion work—you speak each other's language of affection and passion. Sometimes the affection is sweet and tender,
but you also feel there's real sexual passion between you.

When I talk about affection, I'm not just talking about physical affection—hugs, caresses, kisses, that sort of thing. That's important, but the other important thing is the whole atmosphere
of affection. Everything from compliments to cuddling. Pet

names, maybe. Teasing, if that works for you. Sometimes there are joking little insults that totally work as affection for some couples. But affection has to be there consistently, and without effort, and it has to be genuine, not a papering over of anger and distance.

> THE GUY SPEAKS: *"I think we guys get a bum rap, like we just want sex. But at this point in my life [this guy was 30] I really need affection in a relationship. In sex, too. It just makes the whole thing feel right."*

To show you how important affection is, it's one of the first things I look for when couples come to me with problems. Even if their relationship has taken a real hit, if you can also feel that there's real affection, that's a very good sign.

Affection doesn't mean you're drenched in it every minute. That would be icky. But it is there consistently. Not like a waiter who hovers at your table, but like a waiter who somehow always manages to show up at the right time.

Different people need very different levels of affection. And different things mean affection to different people.

But you can't say you have chemistry unless you can say, "I feel there's real affection here."

Is this what you have with your guy? If not, there's no chemistry.

You're probably wondering when I'm going to start talking about sex. Well, here goes.

There also has to be real sexual passion—a sense at the beginning of your relationship that you can't keep your hands off each other. When you make love there's

something special going on much of the time, both physically and emotionally. Later, once your mad-love phase passes, there's still a sexual connection, and you act on it.

Is this what you have with your guy? If not, there's no chemistry. The drop-off in your passion level from the mad-love phase shouldn't be too great. It's kind of obvious: if you don't feel hot and horny for each other when things in your relationship are still developing, when will you?

An important part of this is that you can be honest with each other about your sexuality. And when you're honest, the differences between you that come out don't throw up any big obstacles you can't deal with. I've never met a couple who didn't have differences in their sexuality, even among couples with the greatest sexual chemistry. One person always wants to have sex a little more often than the other. One always wants to do things the other doesn't want to do. One always wants to go faster than the other.

What matters for your sexual chemistry is whether your differences have much of an impact. For example, I know one couple where the guy really wanted to have sex three times a week and the woman found it hard to want to have sex more than once a week. This actually was a big problem for them because they were very rigid about their preferences. When I suggested that they compromise on twice a week, he said, "Wait a minute. There's a huge difference between two and three times a week."

Okay. For him there was. But let's be clear. This is not about the difference between two and three times a week. This is about sexual chemistry. With other couples I've heard things like, "One, two, three times a week, whatever, we can sort it out."

With good sexual chemistry real differences don't seem to be that big a deal. It's the chemistry, not the differences, that tells the tale.

There are plenty of couples who don't see the importance of sexual chemistry. They're such good friends, or there's so much respect, or there's some area of life where they click so well that they ignore the fact that their sexual chemistry is lame or missing.

Or else they just rationalize it by saying that, well, sex is really just a small part of life. But sex is only a small part of life if it's a small part of *your* life. For some people, sex really isn't all that important. If that's honestly the way it is for both of you, then that's fine. You sure don't need to have more sexual chemistry than you both want to have.

For most people, though, you can't say you have chemistry unless you can say there's as much passion for each other as you want.

Dimension 5: You feel there's real mutual respect.

You need to feel that you respect him for who he is and what he's doing with his life. Not who he *could* be, but who he actually *is* right now. And you're confident that he respects you, too, so much so that he brings out the best in you.

If you want to send shivers down the spine of a couples' therapist, bring in a couple who have contempt for each other. Not anger. Contempt. Contempt is a barrage of statements like "There you go again; you always say that," "Why don't you just get your act together?" "Fine, you are what you are. I give up!" The spirit of contempt is more important than the actual words. Whatever form it takes, contempt is about as bad as bad chemistry gets. Contempt is the arsenic of love.

No wonder respect is so important. But I'm not talking about thinking your guy is the most wonderful, successful guy in the world. That's not necessary. You need to be able to see his warts—he's not all that ambitious, he procrastinates, he's a little lazy. *And yet you still respect him.*

The signs. It's not for me to tell you what makes you able to respect a guy. For one woman it's knowledge, for another it's power, and for another it's success. But here are some important questions to answer:

When you look at your guy as a whole, do you feel he has his act together?
Do you feel he's neither stupid nor clueless nor rudderless?
Do you feel he has good values and acts on them?
When life sends trouble his way, does he rise to the occasion?
When you get into one of your crazy places, does he stay sane?

Is this what you have with your guy? If not, there's no chemistry. And just think about what it means if you don't respect him.

If you don't respect him now, then even if he's sweet, even if he's as nice to you as nice can be, even if you feel as sorry as hell for him, even if you're all motivated to fix him up and make him the man you know he can be one day, your fundamental lack of respect will eat away at your chemistry until nothing's left. You won't feel safe with him and your contempt will soon mean that he doesn't feel safe with you. Sexual chemistry is an early casualty of lack of respect. Things won't be easy and comfortable because your intimate space will be littered with eggshells of contempt.

And please understand that it's not respect if you say you respect him for what he could be, should be, maybe will be one day if you help him get his ass in gear. It's only respect if you respect him today as he actually is.

Respect is a two-way street. It's just as important that you feel he respects you. Now you can't lift up the top of his head and peer inside to see if he really respects you. All you can know is how you feel based on the way he treats you, whatever stage of your relationship you're in.

The signs. Okay, he thinks you're cute. But does he *treat* you in a way that makes you feel that he thinks you're stupid or clueless or rudderless? You know, like if you're doing something, does he just barge in and take over? Does he talk to you in a patronizing way, the way you talk to an idiot? When you have something to say that's important to you, does he listen? If not, that's not respect, and it's not good chemistry.

I'm sure you have a friend who respects you. She knows your flaws too, but think of how she treats you. If the way your guy treats you feels like disrespect compared to *that*, then you have your answer.

But respect goes even further than that. There should be something about the way he treats you that makes you a bigger and better person instead of someone cramped, curdled, and corroded. It could be nothing more than a talent your guy has for getting out of your way when you're doing your thing—no wonder you feel respected by him!

What are the best things you have going for yourself? Kindness? The ability to manage a group of people? Being there for your friends? Organizing things when there's a mess? Being happy? You tell me.

When your fit feels right, this relationship will bring out the best in you.

This is a big deal. Lots of guys panic like abandoned toddlers when the women in their lives get caught up in whatever makes them feel they're at their best. These guys tell them, "You're too busy—why don't you relax more." They try to make the women feel guilty for neglecting them. They have subtle little ways of making women feel put down for what they're doing, like saying, "When do you plan on finishing your little project?" It's the word *little* that's a tip-off of fundamental disrespect.

But when there's real respect, you can actually feel yourself basking in the sun of your being your *best* self.

Is this what you have with your guy? If not, there's no chemistry.

Assessing Your Overall Chemistry

The five dimensions of chemistry are determined by your feelings. That means it's completely up to you—no one can tell you whether you have them or not. If you do, you do. If you don't, you don't. And you probably know it.

But what if you're like some women, who say, "I just don't know how I feel about him." What's going on here?

If we sometimes don't know how we feel, it's not because we have a feeling deficit. It's because we have a feeling surplus. We're flooded with feelings. We have a whole three-ring circus of feelings all going on at the same time. "Part of me feels . . . but then another part of me feels . . ." So in fact we do know how we feel from moment to moment. We just don't know how we feel *on average*. We can't read the chemistry because we don't know what all our feelings add up to.

The one-month method. A great way to deal with this is the *one-month method*. Every day for an entire month pay attention to how it felt *that day* to be with your guy, focusing on each of the five dimensions. Keep a record on your calendar or in your Palm Pilot. You can use plus or minus signs. A plus sign would mean "It would be okay with me if the rest of my life with my guy were days like today. I felt at ease and close and safe. We had some fun and there was affection. And I could tell we respected each other." A minus sign would mean "I wouldn't want to be with him if every day from now on were like this. One or more of the five dimensions were low." It's got to be one or the other, plus or minus. Then add up your pluses and minuses at the end of a month. You'll probably be surprised to find there's a lot

more of one than the other. *That's* what all your feelings add
up to.

If you strongly feel that you've got all five dimensions going
for you, that's great. If one or more of the dimensions feels
weak, that's a bad sign. Remember, it's just pass/fail.

Just think about what it means when one of the five dimensions feels below par.

"We have lots of chemistry, on our good days. The thing is,
I don't feel safe with him. I just don't. So there are problems,
but . . ."

That's chemistry? You've got to be kidding me. Without a
sense of safety, this relationship will inevitably fall into a state of
fighting and distance.

"Things aren't bad between us. I just wish things were *easier*
between us. Like when we talk about things, it's always so heavy
and awkward."

Is that chemistry? How can it be? Without ease, a couple just
grows apart.

"The sex—oh my God, it's just amazing. We can't keep our
hands off each other. And it's weird because we felt that way
from the minute we first met at that party. I just wish he took
me seriously. He's not interested in a single thing I have to say.
All we have is our sexual chemistry."

Sexual chemistry is great. But so is mozzarella. So what? You
could have all the mozzarella in the world and you still wouldn't
have a pizza. You could have all the sexual chemistry in the
world and you still wouldn't have real relationship chemistry.

"You know, we're really good friends. Best friends. We talk
about everything. There's such a nice, easy flow between us. So
that's perfect, right? Well, it should be. But our sex life has
fallen off big time. There's no real physical side to our relationship anymore, and we've only been together eleven months. He
says that it's all me, that I just don't want to have sex. You know,

maybe that's true. But I think . . . I don't really understand it but there's something about the way he makes love to me that makes me not want him."

When you look at what's missing, you'd have to say there's a real problem with this couple's chemistry. When affection and sexual chemistry aren't there, there's anger and emptiness and the two people have trouble staying connected.

Predicting the Future of Your Relationship

If one or more dimensions is weak or missing, some hard decisions need to be made.

There will be problems in your relationship later that will grow right out of any dimension that's now weak. This is how the five dimensions of chemistry can predict the future of a relationship.

Suppose in one relationship the fun dimension of chemistry is weak. They don't have much fun together. I'll make a prediction. If they do commit to each other, five, ten, fifteen years from now the part of the relationship they'll be least satisfied with will be the dimension of fun. They'll be complaining that the relationship is stale and boring.

But if all the dimensions are pretty good—they don't have to be great, just pretty good—then you have a solid predictor of a happy future together.

Taking Your Time

It takes time to get a full read on your chemistry. If you move too quickly, it's a little like thinking you love living in Vermont after just a summer there. Only when you've lived there for all four seasons can you say you've had a full experience of the full chemistry, good or bad, between you and Vermont.

So does that mean you can't say anything about your chemistry until you've had all this experience? No. Suppose it's just your first day in Vermont. You still have to go by the feel of the fit. If one day feels good, that means the chemistry's good enough *for you to continue checking it out*. If it doesn't, it's not for you.

So what about you and your guy? You don't know what the chemistry really is until you've reached the point where you no longer need to impress each other. Until you've started sharing everyday life, like going food shopping together. Until you've gotten mad at each other. And, most of all, until you've felt safe enough to put your heart on the line—to show who you are and how you really feel.

Until you experience each other fully as real people in the midst of your real everyday lives, you can't say that your chemistry is as good as you think it is.

If the feel of your fit is *bad* at the beginning, do not pass Go, do not collect $200. It's over. But if your chemistry seems good at the beginning, that's a good sign, but only that you should take the next step. It's worth moving forward, but you're not ready to sign on the dotted line yet.

Suppose after a good period of time you do have a sense that, holy smoke, we've got some good chemistry here. That's enormous. It's your best, your only, sign that you're in the right relationship with the right person.

Bottom line

If you want to know if your guy's Mr. Right, check out the chemistry. There are five dimensions—ease and closeness, safety, fun, affection and passion, and respect—and you shouldn't commit to him unless you have all five dimensions going for you.

CAN YOUR GUY
MAKE THE FIRST CUT?

There are lots of things that can make a guy right for you—the dimensions of chemistry show you the top five. But what are the *fastest* ways to know for sure if your guy's *wrong* for you? There are two: if he's fingernails-scraping-on-the-chalkboard annoying, or if he's got serious personal problems. Let's take these one at a time.

THE MOST ANNOYING MAN
IN THE WORLD

Ask yourself if your guy annoys you. Because if he does, that's going to have a huge impact on all five dimensions of your chemistry.

Annoying, obnoxious, exasperating, pain-in-the-ass guys do to chemistry what slow leaks do to balloons. In my years as a couples therapist I've seen good chemistry survive betrayal, abuse, tragedy, incompatibility, insanity, termites, alien abductions, you name it. But I've never seen chemistry survive when the woman finds the guy annoying. Let me put it this way. Bill Gates is the richest man in the world. Even if he were also the handsomest, sweetest, sexiest guy in the world, if you were in a relationship with him and you found him annoying, you'd still end up saying, "Let me out of here!"

You might think you can suck it up, but you can't. Being with an annoying guy is like living downwind from a pig farm. There's no way you can get used to it.

Here's how Ann, 36, described it. "Brad is a really good guy. A sweet guy, really. That's what makes this so hard. He's also the most annoying man in the world. [Every woman I talked to for whom this was an issue described her guy as "the most annoying guy in the world"—it's what being with an annoying guy does to you.] It's not like Brad has just one or two little irritating traits. I could live just fine with a guy who, I don't know, gargled for twenty minutes every night before going to bed and cracked his knuckles all the time.

"But Brad is like a whole symphony of annoying things. He's still a young guy, but when he sits down he groans, and when he gets up he grunts. Groaning down, grunting up. Like a grandpa. I find myself saying to him, 'Are you going to be getting up and down?' Because I know there's going to be the grunting and the groaning.

"But that's nothing. He's got the worst timing in the world. When does Brad want to make love? you might be wondering. When I'm exhausted, is the answer. God forbid he should want us to have sex when I'm, like, awake. And he's always late for everything. He forgets everything. He hums the same stupid tunes over and over. When he eats, oh God, he puts the fork in his mouth and then scrapes it on his front teeth when he's pulling the fork out of his mouth. He puts his finger in his ear and then looks at his finger. He wears his pants too high. . . . I could go on and on."

Now here's the rest of the story. Ann said Brad was a good guy. He was also good-looking. He had a lot of great friends. He made a good living. He was even a pretty good little lover, except that when he reached orgasm he always said, "Oh, mama!"

So Ann stayed in a relationship with Brad from the age of 31 to 36. That's *five years*, and in the last three years Ann felt that Brad was annoying enough to kill. But she stayed because of his good qualities. She stayed because she thought she loved him. She stayed because she thought maybe she could get used to his being the way he was. She stayed because she hoped she could get him to change.

Your trying to get him to change is the last stage in a relationship with an annoying guy. He "tries" but is unable to change. You fight. He makes you feel like an idiot for making a big deal about little things. "Okay, so you're saying I can stick my finger in my ear; I just can't look at my finger. And *then* you'll be happy?" You fight more. Soon your relationship is consumed by these kinds of fights.

You'd be a damned fool to commit to a guy you find annoying. Whatever you find annoying, if your guy does it, he's toast.

THE GUY SPEAKS: *"If there's something I do that's annoying, I'd rather you said something to me about it instead of just dumping me. Maybe I can cut it out. But you know, I probably can't. And I've got to say that one of the things I found most annoying is being in a relationship with a woman who's always trying to change me. So I guess, yeah, if you find me that annoying I'd rather you dumped me than we just fought all the time."*

After we've gotten seriously involved, we rarely break up with annoying boyfriends just because they're annoying. We should, but we don't. We break up with annoying guys because their obnoxious habits lead to horrible fights, incredible anger. It's sad—like watching love get cancer and die.

What a waste. *Don't cheat yourself—you can do a lot better.*

You deserve to be with a guy who doesn't annoy the crap out of you. And they're out there, plenty of them.

If your guy's great but he has one or two little annoying habits . . . well, you tell me, does that make him an annoying person? I doubt it. But if he's like Brad in the sense that *annoying* is his middle name, in the sense that annoying is what you think of when you think of him, in the sense that he's just too annoying too much of the time, it's over. Good-bye, *sayonara, hasta luego, auf wiedersehen, arrivederci,* see you, wouldn't want to be you.

And just think about this: if you really loved him, would you find him so annoying?

You have to be particularly careful with this if you're in an early stage of your relationship. Annoying guys can be really insidious. They fly in under your radar and get you to care about them before it fully hits you how annoying they are. I think it's a strategy nature devised to allow annoying people to reproduce.

> **Annoying traits are like a pebble in your shoe. For a while you're just slightly aware of them. That's how you can get trapped into doing nothing about it. But at some point they really get under your skin and cause you pain. That's why you've *got* to do something about it.**

Let's say your guy's a whiner. But when the two of you were just starting out he kept his whining hidden. And as he started revealing his true nature, you found yourself saying, "Well, he really likes me. And when it's just the two of us he doesn't whine very much. And so he's a whiner—I can get used to it."

Oh really? That's like saying you can get used to a pebble in your shoe. So are you saying that you can get used to living with someone who whines all day, whines when he comes home at night, whines on Saturday morning, even whines during sex

("My arms hurt; my jaw hurts"), year after year? And you're telling me that you're going to get used to that? Uh-uh. It just doesn't work that way. Getting used to a guy who's a big old whiner is like saying you can get used to living with the sound of a jackhammer next door 24/7.

The same thing holds true for all his really annoying traits. If you're honest with yourself, you'll see that you can't get used to them. They just grow more annoying with time. All I'm saying is, don't kid yourself—you can do a lot better.

And here's the *other* fastest way to know that someone's wrong for you.

PROBLEM PEOPLE POISON PASSION

I don't know how far back you want to go—James Dean? Hamlet?—but dark, troubled guys have often seemed romantic and sexy. Solid, sane guys? *Boring.* I get it. The guy I lost my virginity to was a dark, troubled artist. Even his gnarly toenails were dark and troubled.

But here's the thing. Sexy as it may be, the whole dark, troubled thing is poison if you want your relationship to, like, *last*. If you have good sexual chemistry with a solid, sane guy, there's a good chance it will last. But if your guy has too many problems, you're just going to have to cut him loose because his problems will eventually poison your chemistry.

In today's real estate market, people love fixer-uppers. Unfortunately, that's how too many of us think about the guys we're involved with. Yeah, he likes to gamble and gets in trouble with it. Yeah, he's got a temper and has blown up at a boss and has gotten fired. Yeah, he's bipolar, and it's mostly under control as long as he remembers to take his meds. But with you he's sweet and sexy, and besides, no one's perfect. Plus, you've got an ace up your sleeve. You're going to improve him. Help him. Offer him a safe harbor in your loving arms.

This idea that you're going to be able to change your guy, or at the worst put up with his peccadilloes, well, it's romantic but it's wrong.

It's like always betting on the long shot at the track—a good way to go broke in the long run. And that's what happens to women who get involved with guys who have problems: we go broke emotionally. It may not happen today or tomorrow, but it will happen. Sooner or later we find we're putting out tremendous effort just to keep our head above water, and yet we rarely get anything for it.

What about the fact that your guy has a lot of good things going for him, too? Look, I've stayed in some pretty nice hotels. The room can be absolutely big and beautiful, but if you have noisy neighbors or a broken air conditioner, the experience is spoiled, period. And that's what women told me over and over when they get involved with guys who have problems.

Listen, I'm begging you—if you want a fixer-upper, get a house, not a guy.

If you're in doubt, do this. Write down your guy's biggest problems. For example: "Periodically drinks too much and gets mean." "Can't tear himself away from the office." "Keeps losing money in risky investments." "Sweats like a pig, always."

Now ask yourself, what is your life going to be like with a guy like this? Do you like the day-to-day feel of a life with a guy with problems like this? Piece of cake? If not, you'll be better off with someone else.

Here's a way to double-check this. Ask your friends, "What would a guy need to have to make up for having a problem like this?" If you hear things like, "I wouldn't marry a guy like that if he had Bill Gates's money and a Tom Cruise smile," then why would you?

Call me crazy, but I take the marriage vows seriously. In sickness and in health, for better or for worse, et cetera. That's a big commitment. Why load the dice against yourself? Why not load them in your favor by making sure your guy is as solid and sane as possible?

The flip side to all this is that if the two of you have good chemistry, then solid, sane guys can make your life a pleasure. They make good decisions. They take up the emotional slack when things get hairy. They balance out your nuttiness. They make great fathers. They eliminate a huge amount of worry and heartache from your life. If you don't find *that* sexy, you're not ready to make a commitment.

Bottom line

If your guy's annoying or has a significant personal problem, say bye-bye to him *fast*.

Making Sure Your Chemistry's
Not Counterfeit

Kate sat across from me in my office, her face as pale as a cloud-veiled moon. She'd suddenly woken up to the unbelievable fact that at 37, even though she was attractive, charming, sexy, smart, fun, and loving, she still hadn't managed to find a lasting relationship. Sure, she'd been with a number of guys. But these relationships usually lasted about two years. There'd been problems in all of them. They'd all ended badly.

And the thing is that Kate had known from the beginning of each relationship that there was something wrong. Just like in her current one. She knows there's something wrong here, too. And yet she stays. What's going on?

This time her guy's a writer struggling to get his career off the ground. There'd be nothing wrong with Kate having a fling with a guy like that if she was 23. We all need to have a time in our lives for love adventures. Preferably as early as possible. But Kate's 37 and she wants to have a family. This guy can barely support himself. How can she feel safe with him? Plus, Kate's a project manager for an international relief organization. Every day she talks to interesting guys doing important things. These are the kinds of guys Kate says she wants to marry.

Kate says that she'd been looking for someone for many months after she broke up with her previous boyfriend. So when writer guy showed up at some party, she was ready to jump on whatever opportunity came her way and he was it. He was handsome. He was "interesting." He said he would teach her how to play the guitar. Best of all, he really liked her. So she got swept up in her impulse to be with this guy. "I just want to enjoy the experience," she said.

Does this make any sense to you? Kate's a woman who wants to get married and start a family. Here comes a guy who doesn't want this; nor would she want him as the father of her children.

Kate knows the fit doesn't feel good. Staying with writer guy was like seeing an incredible pair of shoes going for an unbelievable price and buying them *even though they're three sizes too small*. That's not chemistry. That's impulse—taking a need of the moment and hitching it onto a sliver of something you're interested in. And going on impulse is one of the ways we fall victim to counterfeit chemistry.

Counterfeit chemistry happens to the best of us. And if you and I get involved with a guy when there's counterfeit chemistry, it can cause us a lot of problems. At a minimum, you waste years—hanging around to see if you can fix things, hanging around to see if you can stand hanging around, trying to get out, licking your wounds, and then trying to find another guy. Plus every time you go through this cycle you get more discouraged.

But if you know what counterfeit chemistry is, you can save a lot of wear and tear on your heart, and a lot of time as well. So what *are* the forms of counterfeit chemistry? Are any of these present in your relationship?

WHAT TO WATCH OUT FOR

Not being yourself. If you want an accurate reading of your chemistry with your guy, you have to be yourself with him. But aren't we doing that already? The more I talked to women, the more I uncovered an amazing story.

As women, we've lived through a social revolution in the last thirty years. We have more freedom, more opportunities, more choices, and a better sense of ourselves than ever before. This is all good. I don't want to give any of it back. But you can't make an omelet without breaking eggs. And one of the strongest, most common sentiments women shared with me was that it feels damned hard to show who we really are.

Today *the heart is the new virginity.* More and more of us are holding back our deepest thoughts and feelings, dreams and memories, fears and hopes—what we feel are the most vulnerable, most precious parts of ourselves—until we're ring-on-finger, house-in-both-names sure of the guy.

How did we get to this place?

For one thing, a whole decade has been added to our youth. Instead of being a time for settling down, our twenties are a time for drifting and experimenting. And this applies to relationships as well. Why not, we think, have flings with guys who are clearly not husband material?

There's also more sexual freedom in our relationships. Women today have had more sexual partners than women at any other time in history. Compared to our grandmothers, most of us are sluts. This means we're able to get more deeply involved in relationships before we marry. More sex, more intimacy, and more experience mean that we have many more wonderful memories when we finally walk down the aisle.

But we also have darker memories from all the relationships that didn't work out. Unless we've been pretty sheltered, by the time we're thinking seriously of committing, most of us have seen half a dozen relationships go kerflooey on us. We've had our hearts broken at least as many times. We've dated a number of guys who turned out to be duds.

Our ability to trust gets hurt in all this. There were many signs one guy was a loser—his moodiness and anger, his insensitivity to your needs, his women "friends" you knew were more than that.

But you didn't read the signs, and now you find it's hard to trust yourself. "What kind of an idiot allows herself to . . ."

In another relationship there were no signs at all. The guy seemed great, period. Then you got engaged or moved in together and he turned on you, like milk that goes sour overnight. And so you now find it's hard to trust men.

Going through the Relationship Wringer has been quite a ride.

Now add in the high divorce rate. It's much more common than it used to be for first marriages to fail and to fail earlier. Lots of these marriages come to be seen as trial marriages— "Hey, it didn't work out so we decided to move on," not that it wasn't painful. And even if we happen to be one of the minority who've had relatively short or placid dating histories, we know our friends' scary stories all too well. And more women today have divorced parents than ever before.

What's the result of all this? Imagine pushing off from a dock in a new boat when every other boat you've been in has sunk. How could you not be scared? A disappointment here, a surprise there—suddenly you approach every relationship with the wariness of Bambi's mother stepping into the open glade.

> THE GUY SPEAKS: *"Most women I go out with are as nervous as cats. Even when they play it cool. It's like they think I'm going to hurt them, so they just hold back until . . . I don't know until when. I hate it. Yeah, I'm not interested in some chick suddenly getting all needy on me. But I really do want her to show her real self to me. Because that's the only way I can feel safe with her."*

How could we not be so self-protective? Tina, 25, spoke for many when she said that her greatest fear about men was "that they'll just stop loving me."

Here's how Jamie, 32, put it: "How many times can you open

yourself up to a guy, tell him your secrets, show him who you really are, let him inside your dark places, and then face the fact that he's suddenly not calling, or he's seeing someone else, or he's turned into a jerk, or he's using what you've confided to him against you, or he needs more time, or he's not ready, or some other bullshit? You just feel screwed over and hurt. After you go through that a few times you . . . at least this is true for me, I feel, Hey buddy, if you want to see what's in my heart deep down, I'm going to have to feel we're in a real permanent, committed relationship."

No wonder so many of us are virgins of the heart, feeling gun-shy and self-protective in our developing relationships. But here's the thing. *Your number one priority has got to be discovering if your guy's right for you.* That's the only way you can avoid ever getting hurt again. So you're going to have to take a risk. There are no two ways about it. You're going to have to open up your heart and mind to him and show him who you really are.

You just can't tell if there's chemistry between you and your guy until you know how he behaves when he's with the real you.

Anything other than the real you will create fairy-tale, counterfeit chemistry that will one day come crashing down around you. Now here's the good part. If you show who you are right down to all the dark places and you still have good chemistry, you can be incredibly confident that your guy's Mr. Right.

Anyone but him. When Terri was 28 she was just coming out of a confusing, difficult relationship with Al, a struggling independent filmmaker. He challenged her in exciting ways—for example, they worked on a number of creative projects together—and they had amazing fun. But Al was self-absorbed, moody, and not interested in making love with Terri as often as she wanted. In spite of the positives, this was ultimately a demoralizing relationship. It was like a drug where the highs are great but the low times convince you that you have to get off the drug.

When Terri was getting fed up with Al, she met Tom. Compared to Al, Tom was nothing to brag about. He did consumer research in the marketing department of a large company. They didn't do creative projects together. He was just a good, decent guy. But he was very supportive of Terri and very secure and happy with himself.

After Al, Tom was like a drink of fresh, cold water after a trek through the desert. But there were problems with Tom. He and Terri didn't have that ability to just talk and talk in a fun, free way that she'd had with Al.

Terri stayed with Tom and in fact lived with him for three years before she realized their chemistry was counterfeit. *It's not chemistry just because the next guy in your life solves some problem you had with your ex.*

> **If you're with your guy because of the contrast between him and your ex, and not because of who he is in himself, you're setting yourself up for trouble.**

Suppose your ex was always broke. Then the next guy you meet has a lot of money. That can be very exciting. But if the thrill comes *only* because your new guy has a lot of what your ex lacked, it's counterfeit chemistry.

Only one reason to be together. Back in high school and college, all you and I would need was one reason to get involved with some guy. Cute smile. Or six-pack abs. Or you knew going out with him would piss off your parents. Or he had a cool car. Or you'd always wanted to be with a Black/white/Asian guy. *Or he asked you out.* Whatever. Come on, you and I know there's no reason too stupid for us to be with a guy, at least until we know better. Then you ride the relationship until it collapses out from under you.

This is counterfeit chemistry because it's a relationship based on one incredibly narrow concept, like basing a feature-length movie on a *Saturday Night Live* sketch, and you know how well those usually turn out. As long as you can stare at his cute smile or enjoy the sex or appreciate how much money he has or how many cool friends he has or whatever, yes, the chemistry seems great. There's one good reason to be with this guy and everything else is a question mark, *but you need everything else.*

Hypnotized by the one thing they have going, many women stay in the relationship until things inevitably don't work out. Does that make sense? Suppose you went to a restaurant and there was an unbelievably good appetizer. You'd be psyched for the rest of the meal. But then suppose the main course comes and it's terrible. The dessert is a disaster. Do you go back to that restaurant for dinner again? I don't think so. You might pop in just for appetizers from time to time, but that's it.

It works the same way with your guy. If all he's got going for him is that he's fantastically entertaining, then he might be good as a friend, but it will get very old very soon if you're trying to make a life with him. Think of how entertaining he'd have to be to make up for the fact that the sex isn't good, or that he doesn't listen to you or care about your feelings, or that he's completely irresponsible.

These Johnny-one-note relationships only lead to heartache. There are many dimensions to your personality—you deserve a relationship with five-dimensional chemistry.

Analysis paralysis. Many of us overanalyze every shred of information we have about our guy. We go over and over this in our minds, then we hash and rehash this with our friends, fueled by coffee and self-doubt.

"Josh called today." "What did he say?" "I was tied up. He left a message." "Okay, what was the message?" "It was weird. It was pretty much 'Hi, it's me. Just checking in. Call me when you get a chance.' " "What did he mean 'just checking in'?" "I know, that freaked me out. What's with this 'checking in' business? Am I suddenly his mother? Is calling me suddenly a duty thing?" "Wow, I don't know. Did he say 'I love you'?" "No." "Well, he'd been saying 'I love you.' Now he didn't. I don't know what's going on, but I don't like it."

This is just one example of analysis paralysis, and it leads to a dangerous form of counterfeit chemistry. Here's how it works. *We get so involved analyzing our relationships that it actually provides the illusion that it's a worthwhile relationship.* We feel so smart. There's so much to talk about with our friends. The relationship always provides new grist for our mill. It's like falling in love with the movie review instead of the movie.

Like all forms of counterfeit chemistry, the danger is that you could be stuck with two little kids, or in menopause, when it finally gets through to you that the relationship hasn't worked out.

And after a couple of relationships have collapsed like this, it really does a number on your self-trust. I think it's tragic that we get into relationships on the basis of counterfeit chemistry and then, when they don't work out, lose our self-confidence. It's like giving up shopping because someone once foisted a phony hundred-dollar bill on you.

Analysis paralysis is a good way to drive yourself crazy, and when it comes to seeing if someone's right for you, it's exhausting and it doesn't help. The truth is in your chemistry. If your chemistry's not good enough for you to feel it clearly and strongly, then maybe there's not enough chemistry there.

Compatibility. I call them good-on-paper couples—they got together because they seemed to be terrifically compatible. But in fact they end up being *casualties of compatibility*. Two people who met at a party and discovered they'd both been in the Peace Corps in West Africa and still longed to go back and help. An artist in love with his genius meets a woman who's also in love with his genius: "Wow, we both think I'm great, let's get married." And so on.

What happens—and my case files are filled with examples—is that these couples are blinded to their lack of chemistry precisely because they are so compatible. That's what makes them casualties of compatibility. A relationship will collapse if it's based on compatibility without chemistry. The illusion that they were right for each other led them into a relationship that couldn't work and in fact didn't. They just had counterfeit chemistry.

Now here's the thing, and I can't stress it more strongly. I've never had a couple come to me for help who started out with great chemistry and the chemistry just up and died all by itself. Chemistry doesn't work that way.

This is actually good news. It means there are a lot more guys out there who might be great for you than just the thirty-seven guys scattered all over the world who perfectly fit your compatibility profile. And all kinds of surprises are possible, because you just never know who you're going to have chemistry with.

Look, I hope you have terrific chemistry with your guy. And if you do, don't worry about the little ways you might not be so compatible. Your good chemistry will take care of whatever friction might arise from that. But if it turns out that he's not your Mr. Right, then the next time you're out there looking for someone, don't get too hung up on finding perfect compatibility. Cast your net wider. Give yourself a chance to meet more guys, and different kinds of guys. That way you have more of a chance of finding a new guy with whom you have great chemistry.

The wrong guy for the wrong reason. Every day, women commit to guys for very bad reasons. "Bad" in the sense that the chances are that if you commit to a guy for these reasons, you'll end up with a bitter breakup. But along the way, each of these bad reasons leads to counterfeit chemistry.

Some of these bad reasons are so common and so pernicious that it's worth bringing them out in the open.

"Because I was ready." In my experience, this happens a lot. A woman goes along, she's 23, 28, 31, and the whole time she's just not ready to get serious. Maybe she's busy starting her career. Maybe she just wants to explore and have fun. Then suddenly—and maybe she's only half aware of this—she's ready to make a commitment and settle down. And it's the guy she happens to be with when she's ready who seems like Mr. Right—tag, you're it. But here's the thing. You could be as ready as a whistling teakettle and that still doesn't make the guy you're currently with Mr. Right. Don't waste your readiness on Mr. Wrong.

"Because he asked me." Lots of us fall victim to the timing of a guy's interest in us. The relationship enters its romantic phase, and surprisingly the guy pops the question. If a woman's been with guys who've dumped her or been unwilling to commit, she can be so flabbergasted by this move that she'll say yes. But as flattering and reassuring as a proposal is, there's only one good reason to commit to a guy: you think the chemistry is good. The fact that someone wants to commit to you doesn't necessarily mean that he thinks the chemistry's right. And even if he does think the chemistry's right, your being great for him doesn't have anything to do with his being right for you.

"Because he likes me." I can't tell you how sad I was after Amy, 28, and Phil, 36, left my office after their first session. They'd been sent by their clergyman for a premarital assessment. I asked Amy her reasons for wanting to marry Phil. Smiling like the blushing bride-to-be that she was, she said, "Well . . ." and I was waiting for her to reel off a list of Phil's good qualities. Instead, she said, "Because Phil really likes me and we really get along and, uh, he likes me . . ."

As we talked, my heart sank. I had the sense that Amy couldn't face the question of whether she really liked her future husband. Again, the only reason for you to commit to your guy is that your chemistry is great. Then you'll feel that you really like and love him. Sure, it's a relief that he likes you, too. But his liking you is not a reason for you to marry him.

"Because I'm thirty-five." It's not just about the biological clock, although that's huge. It's also about the sense many of us have that the older we get, the harder it is to find Mr. Right.

This is actually not true. Do you hear me? *Not true.* What *is* true is that the older we get, the less likely most of us are to move in circles where available men are floating around. But there are still plenty of available men. They're just not floating around. You have to look for them, like through friends and family, online dating services, and activities you're interested in.

THE GUY SPEAKS: *"Every time a woman says to me, 'Where are all the good men?' I just want to laugh. Where are we? We're running around looking for good women! We just don't know how to find you or meet you or anything. Most single guys I know [this guy was 42 and divorced] want to be in a relationship more than most single women I know."*

I've found that an attractive, happy, warm, fun woman will find plenty of guys at any age if she's willing to get off her butt and seriously look. Instead of saying that it's hard to find Mr. Right, I think we should switch this around and say: "The older I get, the more important it is for me to find someone I have great chemistry with." The truth is that as we get older, our standards should rise. If you panic, you're only betraying yourself. Thinking you've found your Last-Minute Larry is a terrible form of counterfeit chemistry. Don't cheat yourself—you can do a lot better.

"Because he has money." If you get involved with a guy and find out he's a gazillionaire, that's a definite plus. I'd be very happy if my guy were a gazillionaire. But if a guy's having money really made us happier, how do you explain all the divorces among the private-jet set?

Look, if you've got two guys and you have the exact same great chemistry with both but one has a lot more money, of course go with the one with a lot more money. But great chemistry with a guy with a moderate income always means much more happiness than iffy chemistry with a guy with bucks.

There's one exception to this and, boy, does it require your being completely honest with yourself. For some of us, money and everything that comes with it are really more important than love. If you're like this, then a guy is just someone you have children with, someone you make a life with. Most of all, you want that life to be filled with toys and leisure, to be free from financial worry. You won't be disappointed if you live with and have sex with a guy you don't really have much chemistry with.

If you're absolutely sure you're like this, then what can I say? You've got to go with what's most important to you.

Just be careful that you're not kidding yourself. Here's

what women who've fallen for this temptation tell me. You get used to the money and all that comes with it very fast. You soon take it for granted. Within six months to a year it stops making you happy. That's just a fact. For example, in study after study, people are not made happier by having more money than a comfortable minimum. And in studies of big-time lottery winners, for example, it's almost always the case that six months later they were just as happy (or unhappy) as they were before they won.

On the other hand, no chemistry with your guy makes you more and more unhappy over time. Women who went for the money were sure they knew what they were doing, but they were wrong and later they regretted it.

"Because someday he's going to be great." Committing to someone is one of the ways we make a life for ourselves. So the stakes are too high to buy a pig in a poke. If feeling safe with him and respecting him are important, and they should be, you can't take a flyer on a guy you just *hope* is going to turn out great. Before you put the halo on his head, you need to see real evidence. If he's an artist or an entrepreneur, it's not good enough that you think that what he has to offer is awesome. Other people need to think so too, people who can advance his career. In the long run, most dreamers and schemers are heartbreakers.

DON'T SCREW UP THE CHEMISTRY TEST

We've all had the experience of having to take a medical test and the doctor says that we can't eat this or that beforehand, otherwise we'll screw up the test. Or you're having some imaging done and you can't have any metal on your body.

Well, when you're trying to read the chemistry in your relationship there are things people do to screw up that test. Here's the basic principle. You're not able to read your chemistry properly unless you have plenty of time where it's just the two of you with no distractions and no distortions. This has to be supplemented with time when you're together the way you would be under the actual conditions of the life you're going to lead.

Here are some of the most common ways we prevent ourselves from getting an accurate reading of the chemistry.

With drugs and booze. You'd be surprised at how many couples think they get along great because their relationship floats on a cloud of pot, a sea of Scotch, you name it. Just imagine, your whole relationship being based on a pair of beer goggles. *But what happens when you sober up?* You just can't judge your chemistry if it's distorted by mind/mood-altering substances.

With the time-starved love affair. Lots of couples are so busy they rarely have any time for each other. When they do get together what they're really needing most might be more rest or play than true couple time. So in effect their schedules serve as a buffer, preventing their relationship from deepening. You don't know what your couple chemistry is if you don't have time to be a couple.

You better find a way to get that time now. Couples need time alone together the way we need air to breathe. If you can't find time for each other, you're probably not ready to be in a relationship. And you need that time to get an accurate read on your chemistry.

With crises and other special circumstances. You'd be surprised at how often something like this happens. A woman is just starting to get to know a guy when someone she loves dies or she loses her job. The guy is really there for her and they get close and become lovers. It feels like they have something special because of this bond. But is that true chemistry?

Any time a relationship forms in the midst of some unusual or dramatic circumstance, you can't say that you know your chemistry. You just know your chemistry in the midst of that special circumstance. But grief will fade. Your period of unemployment will end. The mad money he inherited will get spent. The great new condo will get old. Don't think you know your chemistry until your life together looks more like normal life for the two of you.

Bottom line

Make sure nothing is preventing you from getting an accurate reading of your chemistry. Be especially careful of counterfeit chemistry.

CAN YOU DUMP THE DUDS?

Have you ever wondered what's up with those women who seem to have an easy job finding guys who are right for them? Well, now you know part of it. They focus on the chemistry. But there's another important part. They dump the duds. When they see that the chemistry's definitely not there, *boom*, the relationship is over. That way, they've cleared the decks so a better guy has a chance to move in. I know it's not easy to do this. It's scary for many of us. But it's essential if you want to find happiness in love.

It turns out that this ability to dump the duds is more important than you might ever have imagined.

Nikki, 29, didn't get this. Here's how she put it: "Knowing what I know now, if Alex were a guy I was just starting to date, forget about it. We wouldn't get past the second date. But you never know these things right away. I'm the kind of woman . . . somehow I manage to stay in relationships past that period where everyone's on their best behavior, and that's of course when the truth comes out. But then I'm stuck. I just don't break up with guys once I've gotten involved. It's like once I'm in a relationship I just can't bear to let it go."

Nikki's put her finger on one of the most important reasons women today end up with a history of bad relationships. Oh sure, if a guy's a disgusting monster, we dump him, although some women don't even do that. But if he's just a dud, we don't dump him. And that's how we get into trouble.

Most women who have a history of bad relationships do so because their pattern is to hang on to mediocre, go-nowhere, chemistry-starved relationships.

If he's a totally admirable guy in every sense but our relationship with him is a dud—there's not much chemistry—we hang in there anyway. Even though in fact the relationship is doomed. And that's a terribly painful mistake.

Smart women dump duds. That's how they find real love.

THE GUY SPEAKS: *"When you first ran that idea by me—dump the duds—I was kind of shocked. Wow, that's cold, I thought. But the more I thought about it, the more I thought—absolutely. If I'm not getting the job done when I'm first involved with a woman, hell, I'd rather she dumped me—then at least we can move on—than just drag it out until we're both miserable."*

Fran, 32, learned through experience that you have to dump the duds. She was able to say about her so-so boyfriend, "I've lived thirty-two years without that guy, why should I let him rattle my cage? He's not working out. He's history."

Fran revealed the latent power we all have. It's time we took advantage of our power. After all, it wasn't that long ago that we didn't have so much power. For centuries, for*ever,* women felt disadvantaged in the mating game. Waiting for the guy to make the moves, our position had been, "If he's into me, I want him— I just have to get him to be into me." We were hitchhikers on the highway of life. The guy was in the driver's seat and most of us accepted that.

But today we feel very differently. We want to be in the driver's seat. We want to be the ones making the go/no-go decision: "I know you're interested in me, but do *I* want you?"

So we believe we should dump the duds, but then we get caught up in the confusion of a developing relationship and we forget. Or we remember but we don't know how to dump the duds under real-life conditions, like how do you break up with someone a week after you've moved in together or when you're looking forward to a vacation you've planned together? What if he gets fired from his job the very day you've decided to break up with him? (Don't worry: later on I'll show you the best way to dump a dud.) But all this is a distraction.

If your guy or your relationship with him is a dud, you must dump him.

WHY WE SETTLE— AND WHY YOU SHOULDN'T

Not everyone will agree that you should dump the duds. "Oh, come on, give him a chance," they say, as if we're talking about kicking some kid out of the first grade because he's having trouble learning his letters.

And even if we agree in our heads that you should dump the duds, it's easy for our fears to take over. If we find ourselves with a dud, we start doing the math. "Okay, I'm thirty-two. It took me quite a while to find my guy. Yeah, he's not so hot. But he's got some things going for him. And even though I know the chemistry's not really there . . . just think about it. If I break up with him, it could easily take me three, four years before I find someone who's . . . well, who knows if he'd be that much better? But then I'd be thirty-five, thirty-six. I'd be feeling a lot more pressure to have a baby. But we're going to want to have some time just the two of us before the baby comes. And if I don't find someone right away, every time I go out on a date guys are going to be thinking, oh, here comes one of those biological-clock chicks."

This is really a version of the old bird-in-the-hand argument. Some guy is better than no guy, yada, yada, yada. My mother believes this. She says these things sometimes that make me want to scream. Just this morning, talking about the unmarried daughter of someone we know, my mother said, "A bad husband's better than no husband." *No.* No way, not today.

There's just one problem. You and I may know this in our minds, but when we're out there and we've just started seeing someone, or maybe we've been seeing him for a long time, we start to weaken.

We fall victim to our fears—"It's so hard to find someone who feels just right—maybe I should just go along with what I've got here. After all, is it likely I'll find someone much better? And that could take me a long time."

We rationalize the problem—"So he's not so great. Who is? Look, I'm just being unrealistic. This is why they say you have to work on relationships."

We tell ourselves that we're not settling because this person has many terrific things to offer. So we think, why not ignore the fact that there are a lot of problems or that there's not much chemistry or that this is probably not the person we were meant to be with or that we don't see ourselves being with him in the long run.

We see that there are problems but we don't do anything about it. There are all kinds of excuses, including plain old laziness, for just staying with someone we know is a dud.

And one of the biggest excuses is the idea that, come on, you've got to be realistic, and even if the guy's not really right for you, you can still be happy together.

Can You Be Happy with the Wrong Person?

You can't be happy if you're with the wrong person. Of course, the person who's right for you is not going to be perfect. He'll have his share of flaws, and, yes, as time goes by those flaws will cause fights. But those flaws will be part of a whole package that's based on good chemistry, and it's only the flaws in your chemistry that matter.

For example, Ashley, 36, has a boyfriend, Jim, who is an opinionated asshole in the sense that when he thinks he's right . . . well, he always thinks he's right. When they were first going together this was a big concern for Ashley. But they had truly great chemistry—he made her feel safe and at ease, they had a lot of fun together, and they had good sex. He also made her feel he respected her. Even though he'd hold on to his position like a bulldog, he always listened to her and never put her down for her opinions. Besides, when he was most opinionated Ashley thought he was very cute.

So if your guy's your Mr. Right, his flaws will turn out to be nonfatal.

As for being happy being single, the truth is that lots of single women are incredibly happy. They may not realize how happy they really are if they're jealous of their friends who are in relationships. Or they see singles on TV running around madly trying to hook up with someone, so that seems like the way it's supposed to be. They don't realize that singles who are happy being single make for lousy TV.

And that's the thing: the main reason single women are unhappy is that they've panicked themselves into thinking that there's something wrong with being single. But if they just took a deep breath and relaxed for a moment, they'd see they're a lot happier than they thought.

Women who are successful in the Land of Love look past the fear of breaking up, the fear of being alone, and focus on the fact that there is someone out there who'll actually make them happy, but they'll never find him if they stay stuck with a dud.

So let me lay it out for you. You can be happy if you're with a person you were meant to be with, a person who fits you just right. That's obvious.

And you can be happy being on your own, not in a relationship. That's not so obvious, but it's still true.

But you can't be happy if you're with the wrong person. And you know you're with the wrong person if there's bad chemistry or no chemistry.

Women think that if they get involved with the wrong guy, it will all work out right in the end. You'll "work out your issues." You'll compromise. You'll learn to accept each other. You'll work on the relationship. But what we now know about chemistry is that it just doesn't work this way. The differences that exist between all couples become increasingly magnified when you don't have good chemistry. It's infinitely harder to resolve problems when you don't have good chemistry. It's hard to heal hurts and get close when you don't have good chemistry.

So why not just face facts now and dump the duds?

WHAT'S YOUR DIAGNOSIS?

So what about you? Do you have trouble dumping the duds? In case you're not sure, answer these three questions:

Are your closets filled with no-longer-fashionable, ill-fitting clothes you never wear?
Yes _____ No _____

If you were to choose a puppy, would you go for the timid, sad-eyed, trembling little creature huddled near the back?
Yes _____ No _____

Do you have friends who use up lots of your time even though they bum you out and you don't have much in common?
Yes _____ No _____

Am I hearing yeses to these questions? If so, you may be suffering from the number one reason women stay unlucky in love. There's appendicitis, bursitis, colitis. Now I want to tell you about *ICDD-itis*. That's *I-Can't-Dump-Duds-itis*.

Here are the signs for sure that you have this terrible condition:

You've got ICDD-itis if you look back on previous relationships and you just can't believe how much time you wasted with guys who were clearly not right for you and didn't make you happy.

Jess, 34, leaned forward in her chair. "Look at me," she said. "I'm very pretty. Right? You know I am. Guys really like the way I look." Then she threw herself back in the chair. "So how come I'm still single? What's wrong with me? There's nothing wrong with me."

Lots of women like Jess have come to me. Somehow a good relationship has eluded them even though they're terrific. There are different things going on from woman to woman, but one thing is always the same. They've always wasted lots of time in relationships that weren't going anywhere. When I asked Jess to give me the history of her relationships, it went something like this.

"Okay, my last relationship was with Jay. What can I say?

When we were falling in love he was so into me. I never knew a guy who worshipped me the way he did. I was his 'bunny.' I don't know what that meant but it felt good. Then came that period where you sort of relax and get used to each other, where things aren't so intense. That's when Jay turned into a real jerk. He started asking me to *fetch* things for him. We'd both be sitting there and he'd be, like, 'Hey, would you get me a beer?' But it was unimaginable that I would ask him to do that. And then he started in with this nitpicking business. All these little things were suddenly wrong with me. My hair was too short, my boobs were too small, my laugh was too loud. He was suddenly on this campaign to change me. *And* he started getting morose. My sweet guy was turning into a grumpy, complaining jerk."

"And how long were you with Jay after he started behaving this way?"

"I guess about three years."

Three years! Jess knew she was a fool for staying so long. She tried to explain why she stayed. She'd kept remembering the good times. She'd been sure he loved her. She'd kept thinking she should just get used to him. She'd been sure she wouldn't find anyone better. There were always holidays and events planned. And, frankly, she'd been afraid of being lonely. She'd kept telling herself that, well, at least the sex is good.

EXPLODING YOUR EXCUSES

Most women with I-Can't-Dump-Duds-itis come up with excuses like these. These excuses are why terrific women give their lives and bodies to men who won't make them happy and can't meet their needs.

Why can't we see it when a guy turns out to be a dud, when the chemistry you thought was there just isn't? It's our excuses that trap us. It's our excuses that put us at risk of missing out on finding the guy who's right for us. So let's explode them.

Who cares what the good times were—all that matters is if there are good times now.

Love?—what good is it if it's not getting the job done?

You're going to get used to him? If you were going to get used to him, it would've happened already.

There's no one better? There *is* someone better and you can find him.

You'll be lonely? Trust me, you won't be as lonely as you think.

And even if the sex or something else is really good, remember that when the chemistry's not good, eventually all the dimensions of chemistry erode.

So there go your excuses. Your guy's not Mr. Right. He's what's standing between you and Mr. Right.

You also have to see past the excuses the guys come up with for why you should put up with them.

Exploding His Excuses

You're in a developing relationship with your guy. You know what that means? It means he's just *a job applicant*. He's applying for the job of being your husband, your main squeeze. So call me crazy, but if you're looking at a job applicant, I don't see why he should be allowed to make any excuses.

If the pizza guy brings you a cold pizza, it doesn't matter how it got that way. If your guy's a dud, who cares what his excuses are. If you wouldn't marry a guy with a face like a warthog, what do you care if some warthog-looking dude comes up to you and explains *why* he looks like a warthog. Who cares? He's still a warthog.

> **When it comes to deciding if your guy's Mr. Right, excuses don't matter. There are lots of guys who deliver what they promise.**

You've heard all their excuses.

"I promise I'll change." You've got to be kidding me. He's all grown up. He did his changing when he was fourteen or nineteen. It's hard for people to change. And the rarest thing of all is some guy who changes because his girlfriend bugs him. If you can't take him for who he is right now, you can get a better guy.

"But I really love you." And of course you love him. It's love. Looooooove. You know, *loooooooooooooooove.* A force more powerful than an earthquake. So what if the relationship sucks and you feel like crap after you spend time with him? He loves you. In the end, won't that triumph? *No!*

Love is not enough. Let me repeat that.

Love is not enough.

Your guy's saying, "I love you," does you no more good than if your local pizza place has a slogan, "We love you." Yeah, but are their pizzas good and do they get to you hot and fast? It's what he delivers, not his slogans, that matters.

"But you've already invested so much in this relationship." It often seems as though the more you give to someone, the bigger a claim he has. But you have to be careful. Thinking like this can put you in a terrible trap.

It doesn't matter how much you've invested in the relationship—the minute you realize that your guy is a dud, he's history.

At least he should be. Don't cheat yourself—you can do a lot better.

If you fall for this excuse, you may be falling for something guys do when they want you but they don't want to go to the trouble of giving you what you want. They deal with your requests for them to change by dragging their heels, and when you've just about had enough—and he can tell because you're furious—they start giving you a little of what you've been asking for. Just enough to get you to shut up. Just enough to get you to invest in another round until the next time when you're fed up, and then the whole cycle begins again.

But here's their ace in the hole. After a few cycles, you've invested so much that you feel trapped. You're exhausted. You're discouraged. *And you've stopped trusting yourself to take care of yourself.* And then he's got you.

Now you see why it's so important to avoid falling for his propaganda when he says, "But you've already invested so much in this relationship." In fact, there's only one question you should ever be asking yourself in a developing relationship, no matter what stage you're in, and it's only two words: "Chemistry good?" If yes, you're in. If no, you're out, no matter how much you've already invested.

IT ALL ADDS UP

I know it seems incredibly paradoxical—to find a guy, you have to dump a guy. Lots of us can't get past this paradox. But that's the wrong way to look at it. To find a good guy, you can't waste a minute with a dud. I'm sure you've seen women you don't think have much going for them and yet they end up with guys who make them happy. How did they do it? Okay, it's partly luck. I'll admit that. But if you talk to them, you'll find that a big part of it is that when they found themselves dating a dud, they tossed him out on his ear. They had the courage to hold out for someone who would make them happy, and that's how they found Mr. Right.

To show you how important this is, let's do it by the numbers. Suppose you have to put your heart on the line for, say, ten guys before you find the one who's right for you. You know, like having to buy ten scratch cards before you can be sure you'll win anything.

Now if you waste three *years* apiece with ten duds, that's about *thirty* years on average before you find Mr. Right. How do you like those odds? Kind of scary, huh? But if you spend only three *months* apiece with ten guys who are duds, that's only thirty months, or *two and a half* years, before you find Mr. Right. Way, *way* better. Thirty years versus two and a half years. You can't argue with arithmetic. Now you see how important this secret of dumping the duds fast is.

Bottom line

The women who have the greatest chance of finding the best guys are the ones who dump the duds the fastest.

ALL ABOUT HIM

Hot Guys/Safe Guys

Sharon, 38, told me, "There's something about my whole dating history that's screwed up and I can't put my finger on it. There's a certain kind of guy I like . . . they're exciting. They really do something for me. But if I'm so attracted to these guys, how come it never works out? And then I'll get involved with another kind of guy—I call them Mr. Nice because they're real nice—so opposite the kind of guys I usually like. Of course that never works, either. What the hell is going on here?"

Hot/Safe Ping-Pong

One of the biggest ways we confuse ourselves about chemistry is by getting stuck in what I call hot/safe ping-pong.

This is where for a period you go with guys you think are hot. *Hot* could mean *very sexy*. It could mean *incredibly handsome*. It could also mean *fun*, as in, "We have all kinds of fun together." Or hot could mean *totally cool*. *Hot* could also mean *powerful*—lots of us find powerful men really hot. Or *someone who does exciting things*. Maybe *someone dangerous*. Or *someone rich*. The point is that this is a guy who really turns you on, gets your juices flowing.

But you keep getting burned by the hot guys, and when that happens too many times you look for the safe guy, the nice, sweet, harmless, easy-to-control, self-effacing guy, but then that's a disaster because there's no heat.

Hot guys who aren't safe. Safe guys who aren't hot. You can get stuck spending your whole life ping-ponging back and forth like this. You deserve the great chemistry you need and want. You deserve a guy who's both hot and safe, and I'll show you how to make sure you're getting both.

How We Get Hooked on Hot

Judy, 33, is a yoga teacher in Los Angeles with a big problem. She's got a thing for totally gorgeous guys—underwear-ad gorgeous. "I've really tried, really, to go out with guys who are just okay-looking, but they don't do it for me. The problem is that guys who are really gorgeous know it. And this is LA, so most of them are trying to be in show business or are, like, personal trainers who work with people in the business. And I'm not bad-looking by LA standards, but I think a big part of the reason why they go out with me is because I'm a yoga teacher and yoga is hot. I'm, like, the cute yoga teacher. And I'm always afraid of what's going to happen when they get to know the real me.

"The same thing happens over and over. Take my relationship with Dave. I met him through my friend Gigi, who's this men's hairstylist. She does a lot of model/actor-type guys. She's got great access. She's my connection. I get these calls, 'I got this great guy for you.' Plus she's hands off because she's a lesbian. Dave had just gotten a small role on some medical detective show. I think because the show mostly dealt with guts and maggots and brainy investigators, they wanted some stupid, good-looking hunk to play off of. Anyway, when I went out with Dave it was one of those instant chemistry things with us."

Let's pause for a moment and think about that last statement. Was it really chemistry? No, Judy's wrong. It wasn't instant chemistry. It wasn't even instant sexual chemistry. It was just instant *partial* sexual chemistry—she was turned on by the way he looked—but where was the tenderness and affection? And where were all the other dimensions of chemistry?

"It was total passion right away. I think we were each totally the other's type. He was tall, kind of Latin complexioned, with broad shoulders. I think he liked me because, I don't know, I'm thin, cute, bendable, whatever, but we were totally into each other.

"And it stayed that way for a long time. We had to be together every minute. But the whole time I'm thinking this is too hot not to cool down. And I'm waiting for how it's all going to blow up. I mean, I'm sorry, but it's true—it always blows up. For me anyway. It always has so far, right?

"So then Dave gets fired from his show. I guess they'd never intended him to be a permanent character. And he's thinking, 'Oh, I'll get another job right away.' But he keeps making the rounds and months go by and it's all dried up for him. Plus his money is going. The thing is, though, that he just can't go back to waiting tables. *He'd gotten a write up in* TV Guide *as a face to watch.* So his brilliant solution was to get more and more depressed every day.

"The next thing I know he's explaining to me why he's started seeing this chick who's the daughter of this producer. He wants me to *understand*. What we have is still very special. But he can't get tied down, blah, blah, blah. Plus this bitch might be able to help him in his career, blah, blah, blah.

"I was totally devastated. I don't know how to make you get this . . . I'd always had incredible chemistry with everyone I'd been with, but with Dave it was incredible chemistry with special sauce on a sesame-seed bun. We were so hot together. We'd watch TV all tangled up in each other's arms, and we'd go to the beach and people would look at us as the couple everyone wanted to be.

"I don't know what to do. What do you want from me—I like what I like. It's not going to work for me going out with an average Joe. You can hate me for that if you want to. But these guys like Dave are all going to break my heart. Always have. Always will."

Judy's an extreme example of someone setting herself up for the hot/safe ping-pong many of us struggle with.

LOOKING FOR THE HOTTIE

We all want someone who's hot. I get it. Hot is good. But this is also where fast, cheap counterfeit chemistry comes from—you see it, you want it. And if you find someone who thinks of *you* that way too—*boom!* You think you're madly in love. Just the way you've dreamed of. And this is how we become like guys who are attracted to some chick just because she has big boobs. "What a rack! I bet we'll have a great relationship." Stupid, huh? But we do the same kind of thing.

And hey, what's wrong with that?

Nothing, you'd think. It's the way we were back when we were starting out in high school, all dopey and hopeful. In college. Even much later. We just want the thrill. We don't think anything bad will happen to us chasing after the hot guys.

As people grow up a little we sometimes think our tastes are more mature, that we're less interested in someone hot. But too often we're kidding ourselves. We just have a different idea of what's hot. I know middle-aged women who think being a museum curator makes a guy hot!

And in case you think you're not like Judy because you never thought you could get some male-model-type guy—6s can't get 10s, you think—remember that everyone has an attainable version of hot, even if it's just a guy with a motorcycle or a time-share near a beach.

I admit, every once in a while women end up happily married to the hottie who finds them hot, too. It happens. And we're all jealous. But most often it doesn't happen like this.

You need to know that if all you're looking for is hot, that's probably all you'll get.

THE GUY SPEAKS: *"This is going to sound bad, my saying it, but I was actually on one of those top-ten eligible bachelors lists. I made a good living and I was supposed to be sort of good-looking. So that makes me a certified hot guy, right? Well, I had all these women . . . I'm sorry, but they were throwing themselves at me. The fact that I was hot was all they needed to know. And I was like, jeez, let's get to know each other before we start deciding how wonderful the other is. I just felt they were setting themselves up for this really one-dimensional relationship."*

THE PROBLEM WITH HOTTIES

But hot is *not* all you want. Even if you make a huge deal about how you can only be with someone who's incredibly good-looking or whatever, are you telling me that you don't also want someone who's kind and sweet and solid and sensible and supportive and fun? Of course you want things like that. It's just that when you're hooked on hot, you ignore the other parts of the guy. No wonder so many show-biz marriages don't work out. No wonder so many marriages between an older guy who some consider hot because he's very rich and a younger woman who's very beautiful don't work out.

By itself, hot is not enough. Hot can draw you to your doom and then turn into nothing when it cools down.

Here's how dangerous it is to go for the hot guys. I heard an interview with Kirstie Alley last night. She talked about how she was addicted to hot, hunky guys. She got her heart broken by them so many times that *she got fat* to stop the whole dynamic. If she was too fat for the hunks to want her, she was safe from going after the hunks.

Trust me—there are way better solutions. But this is the kind of thing that happens to us when we're hooked on hot.

Many of us continue to look for hot because we need something exciting to get a relationship launched. Some people call it a spark or electricity. And this often comes from the things we find hot about each other. I know a guy in his forties who still cannot *and will not* go out with anyone except tall, exotic-looking actress/model types. His heart's been put through the shredder more times than a Mafia guy's income statements. But he won't back down. Not yet, anyway.

THE FLIGHT TO SAFETY

Now here's what eventually happens when we focus on looking for someone we find hot.

These one-legged-stools of relationships keep collapsing under us, and we get beat up emotionally. We eventually can't take it anymore. We don't want to get hurt again. So we flip.

"This time," we say, "I just want to find someone who won't hurt me. Just a nice, safe, good person." If you've been poor, someone who has a good income will make you feel safe. If you've been with manipulative guys who play yo-yo with your heart, some kind, simple, sincere soul will make you feel safe. If you've been abused, someone who may not seem all that powerful can make you seem safe. Suddenly a relationship for us stops being a place of excitement (one kind of partial chemistry) and becomes a place of safety (another kind of partial chemistry). It's like going from focusing only on whether your pants are the right length to focusing only on whether they make your ass look good. You should be able to have both!

Getting ping-ponged from a series of hot relationships into a safe one happens to most of us. It happened to my mother-in-law, and check out how it turned out. It was a long time ago. She shocked her very respectable family by becoming a dancer—a Rockette, then an apache dancer partnered with a guy named Ramon in a nightclub act. She spent her time with the bohemians in New York's Greenwich Village. The only guys she was interested in were dashing artists and romantic writers. These were her hotties. She even had a long affair with an Oscar-winning filmmaker. Of course these guys were mostly interested in working their way through the cuties who made themselves quite available. So my mother-in-law found herself in a number of tumultuous relationships that ended in pain and disaster. The hotties were killing her.

She reached her breaking point after the filmmaker dropped dead from burning his candle at both ends. She was in her midthirties and her biological clock was keeping her up nights. That's when she settled on my father-in-law. He was an engineer who, as it happened, was still living with his parents. He had little of the heat that the other men she'd been with had. But, as she put it, "I thought he was safe. I knew he wouldn't hurt me." Sure—this shy, decent man thought my sexy, beautiful, exciting mother-in-law was the greatest thing that could ever possibly happen to him. She'd found the guy who wouldn't leave her.

And with that, she once told me, she consigned herself to a small and stifling life with him that at points drove her mad with boredom.

Consider this a warning. This is what happens if you get caught up playing hot/safe ping-pong. You might be lucky, but the overwhelming likelihood is that when you're fried and frazzled after too many exploding relationships with hotties, you'll fly into a relationship with Mr. Safety, hang out there until you're ready to scream, and then maybe bust loose by getting involved with another hottie. I know women who've spent their entire lives going back and forth like this.

I'll bet that you can explain big chunks of your dating history with this hot/safe dynamic.

It doesn't have to be such a dramatic story, either. It could be that a few wild romances in your twenties were enough to make you eager to settle for someone safe and snoozy whom you called normal.

Lots of times the dynamic happens in reverse. People start by being in relationships with someone safe and nice and appropriate, and when they can't take the boredom or emptiness anymore, they bust loose with someone they find hot.

Lots of women have affairs with someone who's the opposite of their husband on the hot/safe meter. More ping-pong, except that now you're playing both sides of the table at the same time.

BREAKING FREE

So how do you get out of hot/safe ping-pong? And how does understanding this help you decide if the person you're with is right for you?

Here's what works: you have to make sure that your guy gives you *enough* of *both* heat and safety.

I know what you're thinking. It was hard enough to find a guy. Now you've got to see if you have perfect chemistry with him in every respect.

No, no, no. I'm not saying that at all. I don't have perfect chemistry in every respect with my guy. None of us does. And we don't need to.

Here's what you should look for. If you get involved with someone because he's high on heat, you have to make sure he also makes you feel safe *enough*. Plus all the other dimensions of good chemistry. If you get involved with someone because he makes you feel very safe, then he's got to be just hot *enough* for you to find him sexy and interesting.

And that's *not* too much to ask for.

How Hot Is Your Guy?

Ask yourself what are the *top three* exciting, fun, sexy, interesting, challenging things about your guy. What are his qualities that get your blood flowing? Make a list.

To stimulate your thinking, here are some things women have put on their lists:

- "We have these great interesting conversations."
- "He always comes up with fun ideas for things for us to do."
- "We like to make love a lot and it's great."
- "He never lets me get away with crap, and I find that very stimulating."
- "He's so good-looking I just want to be with him."
- "He's got a fantastic smile that lights up the room."
- "He's always into something very exciting, and his passion for those things is contagious."

So how about it? When you look at your list that shows your guy at his hottest, how hot is he?

Who Do You Think Is Hot?

If you chose him because he was hot, there are probably some good things on your list. If you chose him because he was safe, you need to be careful. The question you have to ask yourself is, Is your guy hot enough for you? Hot enough for you to feel some sort of electrical spark, some excitement, some challenge?

If your guy just doesn't live up to what you need for a guy to be minimally hot, you won't be happy with him. You'll be bored, restless, and resentful.

Don't pretend your partner is hotter than he is. The fact that he's a nice guy or that you get along or that you manage to go to really nice restaurants together has nothing to do with how hot he is. This is too important an issue for you to cheat yourself—you can do a lot better. If you're with someone you just don't find hot, your relationship *will die* from boredom or lack of interest. And all the excuses in the world won't save it.

Think of it like this. Let's say it's really important to you to lose weight, so you've started a diet. You're going through the market and you plunk some frozen pizzas in your cart because they look so good and they're on sale. As you're wheeling your way to the checkout line, you look at those pizzas with misgivings. You totally know they're not what you want. You totally know if you buy them, you'll eat them. And if you eat them, you'll be unhappy. They just don't meet your minimum standard for diet food.

Now, your guy's just an item in your shopping cart. You haven't hit the checkout line yet. If he's not hot enough for you, you can pop him on some shelf you happen to be passing.

Doing this sounds pretty easy, doesn't it? Who could possibly get it wrong? Well, lots of us get it wrong. Let's figure out why, because it's too important not to get it right.

Here's what we need to remember.

Accept your need for heat. If you've been hurt by being with someone who didn't make you feel safe, then it's easy to go all the way to the other extreme and say that safety is the only thing that matters in your next partner. This is one of those classic ex-to-next issues—issues that come up in your current relationship because of issues you had with your ex. But you want to avoid making the mistake Debra made.

"I'll admit I was one crazy girl when I was in my twenties," Debra, 37, said. "I had this thing for musicians. Any cool-looking guy who played in a band—that did it for me. And we'd hook up for a while and sometimes get really serious about each other. But of course I always got my heart broken, because there were all these other chicks throwing themselves at my guy.

"When my thirtieth birthday was approaching, I hit the panic button. This shit could go on forever, I thought, with me always ending up on the losing end. Now, the whole time my mom had been bugging me to settle down with a nice boy with a nice job. And she was always trying to fix me up with her friends' sons. And they were all, so help me, dentists and computer guys.

"But one day when I was in my panic mode my mom called about this new guy who was supposed to be so handsome, and he was a lawyer—Mr. Perfect, she said. I caved. I thought, Okay, you want me to be with a nice safe guy, I give up. I sure wasn't having any luck with the other guys.

"So I went out with the guy. And the thing is, he *was* kind of handsome in a really boring way. I think that's what hooked me, along with my panic. So I threw myself at him and he never knew what hit him. He'd never imagined being with such an exciting girl. Next thing you know, we were engaged. You could've scraped my mother off the ceiling, she was so happy.

"I think the whole time we were engaged I knew I was making a mistake because this guy was so . . . if he'd been a food, he'd have been processed American cheese. At the engagement dinner he made some speech and it was so lame, that's when I knew for sure. The next thing I knew I found myself making out with one of the musicians."

Debra's an example of what happens when not feeling safe drives you to the other extreme. You become so hungry for safe that you're likely to go overboard. But just because she'd been hurt by a succession of hot-seeming waste-oids, that didn't mean her need for heat wasn't valid.

The most important thing is to keep your focus on what you need to be happy (and if that includes being with a hot guy, so be it), not what you need to prevent the last bad thing from happening to you again.

THE GUY SPEAKS: *"One of the biggest mistakes I ever made was I was involved with this woman and she was nice and kind of pretty actually, but there was something missing. She just didn't turn me on. Not at all. And the mistake I made was I hung in there. She was so nice, I didn't want to hurt her. But of course I did hurt her, much worse, because I wasted a lot of her time."*

Know how much heat you really need. Some people find themselves passing on terrific guys because they think they need more heat than they really do. For example, for Julie, 39, a "hot" guy was someone who was really successful in a prestigious field. The fact that he was, say, an architect wasn't enough for her. He had to be an architect who did important commissions. Plain old doctors didn't cut it. She wanted a doctor who did heart transplants and brought back the dead.

Now occasionally Julie did run into some pretty high-powered guys. Unfortunately most of them were boring, annoying, or nasty. So she wasted many years of her life getting involved with these A-list duds.

The sad part is that what she was looking for had nothing to do with what would make her happy. How does being able to brag about your guy make you feel loved? At one point she said, defending herself, "I have a good job and I need to find someone I can respect."

"Yeah," I said, "but how great a résumé does a guy have to have for you to be able to respect him?"

I got her to agree to spend a year getting to know guys who had a good job and did it well. Nothing to brag about but certainly nothing to be ashamed of. This is a much bigger pool of guys, so it's much more likely that she'd find someone it actually felt good to be with. She resisted at first, using the dread "settling" word: "I don't want to just settle for some nobody."

Yes, settling is bad. But let's define that ugly word that can do so much damage.

> **Settling** is when you're with a guy who doesn't meet your needs and doesn't make you happy but you're with him because you don't think you can do any better.

This kind of settling *is* a mistake. It's based on the idea that something is better than nothing. Wrong! Something you don't like and don't want is worse than nothing. That's why you should never settle.

But it's never settling when you make choices so you can actually get what will make you happy. It might be nice to own a Rolls-Royce, but it's not settling to buy a Camry if it's a car you'll enjoy that you can also afford. So when I say don't cheat yourself, you can do a lot better, I mean don't settle for anything less than someone who will make you happy. It's about happiness, not bragging rights. That's why it's so dangerous to have insanely high standards for who you insist is hot.

When I held Julie's feet to the fire, she realized that it wasn't "settling" for her to be with a guy who had an okay career. On the contrary, she found guys she respected for their dedication and she also opened herself up to a much, much wider pool of guys. She found she was a lot happier and had a lot more candidates looking for "a great guy with a good job" than "a good guy with a great job."

Why do we do this to ourselves—set the bar too high?

Well, why do *you* do it to *yourself*?

One possibility is that you are afraid of intimacy. You're afraid of getting hurt by being in a relationship, either because you're afraid you'll be attacked emotionally or abandoned, or because you're afraid you'll lose yourself in the relationship. If so, then maybe what you're doing is protecting yourself from another person's power to hurt or overwhelm you by setting the bar really high. No candidates, no relationship, no risk. *Is that you?*

Another reason we set the bar too high is narcissism. Some of us find it easier to love the idea of another person than to actually love a real human being. We want bragging rights, not intimacy. *Is that you?*

It may be hard to admit this, but it might be your first step out of a destructive pattern where you keep hooking up with people who can't make you happy. You can't cuddle up with bragging rights.

Watch out for the guys who turn out to be not so hot after all. One thing that happens to many of us is that we start out with a supposed hottie who turns out to be not so hot. How does this happen?

Suppose you're with someone who seemed to be fun and interesting when you were first dating. That's what made him seem hot to you. But now that you're starting to feel a little more comfortable with each other, uh-oh, you find that he does an awful lot of worrying about work. In fact, that's mostly all he does. And it's not because his job is particularly bad.

What's going on? Lots of men have two personalities. The charming Dr. Jekyll appears when you're first dating. He wants you to think he's a fun, interesting, successful guy. But it's hard for him to keep it up because it's not who he really is. When he feels confident he's got you, or when he's just exhausted from playing the role, he turns into the evil Mr. Hyde.

Okay. You got snookered. It sucks. But what we do next is the equivalent of a woman who's gotten mugged running after the fleeing thief so she can also give him her ATM card. We find it hard to accept who our guy has turned into. No, no, no, we say, this creep isn't my real guy. He's . . . working too hard! It's just a temporary mood he's in. Or the ever-popular "It must be my fault."

You will never find the great guys if you fall for this. What you need to accept is that the guy who shows up once your relationship has ripened a little, once he starts feeling he can stop being on his best behavior, is the real guy.

HOW SAFE IS YOUR GUY?

Unless you just came out of a convent, you've probably been hurt in a previous relationship. Lied to. Cheated on. Used. Unceremoniously dumped. Yelled at. Neglected. Criticized and humiliated. Controlled. Robbed. Financially exploited. You name it. And that's just what the decent guys did to you.

Okay, I'm kidding. I'm sure there were plenty of good guys, too, and they didn't do any of these things. It's just that a few rotten no-goodniks can easily spoil the whole barrel.

No wonder safety is a big issue for most of us. And now you look at your guy and you have to be wondering if you're safe or secure. If you're in the early stages, you might be wondering what huge surprises are in store for you. If you're in that sobering later stage where reality starts to set in and you've noticed some warts on him, you might be wondering how big these warts are going to grow.

SO HOW DO YOU MAKE SURE THAT YOU REALLY ARE SAFE?

Make a list of what you need to feel safe with a guy. Make sure you include everything that's important to you. Here are some things women have said:

- "I need a guy who's open. No secrets. Nothing hidden."
- "I need a guy who makes a good living and is careful with his money."
- "I need a guy who won't be starting 'relationships' with other women."
- "I need a guy who isn't a rage-aholic. We all get mad and there's nothing wrong with expressing anger, but anger really scares me and I need to know I'm with someone who has it under control and doesn't get angry too often or too easily."

Now this is important: your safety needs shouldn't just be based on whatever happened to have gone wrong in past relationships. That can be part of it, but your safety needs really grow out of who you are, not your history. If your ex made you feel abandoned because he was working all the time, you're not going to find Mr. Right if you look for a guy who doesn't care about money or success, not if you don't want to worry about making ends meet. If your ex had a porn collection that could fill a U-Haul, you're not going to be safe just because your new guy is relatively porn-free. Make sure you don't focus exclusively on your past disasters, and you'll be okay.

Now when you look at your list of what you need to feel safe and secure, how does your guy stack up? Does he make the grade? Does the real guy that you know consistently deliver what you need? When you look at what you need to feel safe and secure, how do you feel about him? Content? Or queasy?

Stephanie, 27, needed to feel that the guy she was with wasn't going to criticize her at every turn. To be ambushed and humiliated by some random put-down, even if it was supposed to be "helpful," eroded her sense of security. But it was hard to tell about her guy, Bob. They'd been together for only six months and they were still in the stage where everything seemed wonderful. But they'd fallen into a pattern where Bob taught Stephanie a lot of things. It made sense to them. He was older, better educated, more worldly. But she couldn't help wondering if all this "help" wasn't really a prelude to a lot of criticism.

I suggest you do what Stephanie did. Suppose your guy was just a guy you knew really well. Ask yourself if you'd recommend him to your sister. What would you warn her about if she were thinking of getting involved with him? What issues would you say that she didn't have to worry about because you're sure he's safe? When it comes to safety issues, we're much more responsible when we think about others than when we think about our own safety.

Look at your list of what you need to feel safe with a guy. He is not right for you if he makes you feel unsafe or insecure in places where you've just said you need to feel safe.

Solving a Mystery

A mystery I've struggled with—and I'm sure you've wondered, too—is why so many of us end up feeling unsafe in relationships when it's so important to all of us not to get hurt. But there are solutions to this mystery. It's important to understand what's required to guarantee we'll end up feeling safe.

You have to be willing to see what's real. Many of us wear goggles that prevent us from seeing what's real. These goggles usually come from some preconception, some fixed idea that blinds us to the truth in front of us. For example, you might think that it's cute or sophisticated to be in a relationship where there's a lot of verbal sparring. But deep down you might be a person who just can't take being in a relationship with someone who isn't kind and thoughtful about what he says. That's what you really need to feel safe. Put-downs, however sophisticated, make you feel bullied. *You need to respect your need.*

You also can't say, "I know he has a good heart," if you're with someone who puts you down. His "good heart" is cold comfort if you're constantly feeling wounded and abused by the kinds of things he says to you. Take off your goggles and see what's real: you are being put down and it does hurt, whatever he claims his intentions are.

Don't be blinded by his excuses or by the excuses you make for him. Does he make so little money that you wonder if you're going to be able to have a child with him? Well, don't blind yourself by saying, "He's really trying." All the trying in the world won't add up to enough money for you to feel safe.

Does he always flirt with women and maintain relationships with ex-girlfriends? What's your excuse for that? Is it that "He means well"? How can he mean well if he does something he knows hurts you?

You can be with a guy who flirts with women if you want to. You may be someone who isn't bothered by that. But I'm saying, don't deny what it is that bothers you, whatever that is.

And, by the way, I am not saying you should immediately break up with your guy if he's done one little thing that makes you feel unsafe. But you should break up with him if what he does is a big deal for you, you've asked him to stop and you've explained how it makes you feel unsafe, and then he either can't or won't stop doing it.

I once saw a couple where in the first fifteen minutes of the first session it came out that he drove really fast. She let him know how scared she was, but he just laughed. I knew immediately these guys were doomed. Why? Because clearly her needs were nothing to him. And so the future of their relationship was written in stone. Indeed it turned out to be a disaster, a kid and a painful divorce later. Of course it was his fault because he was such a creep. But it was her fault, too, because she saw what a creep he was and went along with him anyway.

Don't blame yourself. Women too often stay in relationships where we don't feel safe or secure because we blame ourselves, not him. We're not understanding enough, or patient enough, or generous enough, we think.

This may be noble, but it's unhealthy. This is a special problem for women with a talent for overthinking things.

Suppose a guy is verbally abusive. You're blaming yourself if you say, "Well, I should be tougher. I'm just going to try and be tougher." Hey, you and I should be a lot of things. But we are who we are. And if being with someone who's got a mean mouth makes us feel insecure, then we have to accept that this is a person who's not right for us, no matter what else he has going for him.

Check it out with your friends. Tell them what he said that hurt you. If they all say that you're being a big baby, well, maybe you should toughen up a little. But if he calls you the *c* word every time he gets really mad at you in spite of your asking him to stop, most people are not going to say that you're being a baby if you say it bothers you. Come on, just think about it— what kind of a guy would keep on saying something like that after he knows how much it bothers you? It's not about what you do, it's about what he does.

Bottom line

Save yourself from ping-ponging back and forth from hot guys to safe guys. Don't give your heart to a hot guy unless you're sure he's safe. Don't give your heart to a

safe guy unless you're sure he's hot. Remember, you deserve as hot a guy as you really want. And no excuses. But no matter how hot he is, if he doesn't make you feel safe and secure, now's your time to get out. It's a lot easier now than after you've married the guy.

Is He a Keeper or a Loser?

Okay, so it's really important to dump the duds. But what makes a guy a dud? Where do you draw the line between a keeper and a loser?

Suppose you're eating out and you order a salad. You start to eat and you realize that the tomatoes are kind of mealy and dry. What do you do? Well, maybe if you're hungry, and if the salad's pretty good otherwise, and if you know you're probably not going to find fresher tomatoes here, you'll go ahead and eat it anyway. But suppose you find a bug in your salad. Will you go ahead and eat *that?* Of course not! After they scrape you off the ceiling, you'll send it back. And maybe even demand a free meal.

So who are the bugs in our love salads? Who are the guys that you have to send back no matter what?

You might think it's funny that I'm even asking this question. After all, you're a smart woman, and an asshole is an asshole. But we do need help with this. Ask Mary, 26. "I'm sorry to be so cynical, really, but here's how they get you. Okay, fine, here's how they get *me*, but it's not just me. It's like Evil Guy X sets you up by sending out a whole bunch of guys for you to date and they're all *total* losers. Bad skin, no hair, mean, creepy, goofy losers. So just when he's gotten you to the point where you're ready to enter a convent, Evil Mr. X himself shows up and you think it's the Second Coming. He's nothing special, believe me, but he seems kind of friendly, kind of interesting, kind of not a gargoyle. Big deal. But it is a big deal because he's better than all the creeps you've been with.

"So you get involved because you're so relieved that he likes you and he's not obviously awful. And I think it's really that relief you're feeling that makes it seem like you actually have chemistry with the Evil Mr. X. Believe me, you don't. Because I've lived through it. You're ignoring the fact that the chemistry's not so hot—which you could see if you just looked—because you're ignoring who he really is, and frankly who you really are. Because of the relief thing.

"Anyway, pretty soon there are cracks in his mask and you start seeing him for who he really is. But you don't see it because you don't let yourself see it. You're afraid of the creeps and you're afraid of being alone and you're dazzled by the little sliver of counterfeit chemistry you have with Evil Mr. X. I don't know about you, but that's how I got involved with a lot of selfish, cold, lying . . . jerks."

I think Mary said it perfectly. Reading chemistry is like driving. You have to be willing to see what's in front of you.

WHAT TO LOOK FOR WHEN YOU'RE DECIDING IF A GUY'S A KEEPER OR A LOSER

If he delivers on his promises, that's a very good sign. If he's a liar, he's a loser.
Let's face it, most guys fib and fudge about little things. And a guy like that isn't necessarily worse than one of those guys who's always on a crusade to tell the truth, because too often Mr. Truth Crusader would rather cut you into little pieces than bite his tongue.

But when I say that a liar is a loser and that you have to dump him immediately, I'm talking about a guy who lies often enough so that you just don't feel you have the ground under your feet with him. You don't know if you're coming or going. You're haunted by lies he's told you in the past. And you're haunted by not knowing which of the things he's telling you now are true. He led you to believe that he graduated from college, when actually he attended for only a year. He led you to think that he had all kinds of money "tied up in investments," when the only thing really tied up was your heart, in knots.

If your guy is a liar, you have to cut him loose.

If he's upbeat and optimistic, that's a very good sign. But if he's Mr. Negative, then it's a negative on your going forward with this relationship.

It sounds so corny—cheerful, pie-eyed, can-do guys. Male cheerleaders. Give me a break. But you've got to listen to the women who know. Grim, glum, gloomy guys are real love torpedoes. They will sink the ship of your affection fast. It's very hard to love a Mr. Negative.

You have to be careful, because a lot of sourpusses hide their true negative selves early on. Then when their negativity starts to come out, it gets expressed as either sadness, which brings out your pity, or realism, which makes you think maybe the guy knows what he's talking about.

But don't get hooked. If your guy's a downer now, when things are supposed to be at their best, what's he going to be like if things are in the pits?

And what about Prozac? What do you do about a guy who's had to deal with depression but is now taking medication for it? Here's the deal. Don't commit to a guy whose depression is not under control. That would be like a swimmer using an anvil as a life raft. But if the guy has had psychotherapy and has been taking antidepression medication for at least a year, and his mood has stabilized in the up position and he doesn't have any side effects to complain about, then it might be worth hanging around if and only if you have great chemistry in all five dimensions. But still this is a guy you want to take your time with before making any serious commitments, just to be sure he really is healthy.

If he's able to learn about how you work and what you need, that's a good sign. But if he starts out clueless and stays that way, he flunks.

If understanding women were a course in school, we think most guys would flunk. It's not that guys are stupid or uninterested. I really think it's because too many straight guys think that understanding women is gay. Plus a lot of guys are lazy and they believe that if they pretend to be stupid about us, we'll let them off the hook, the way we do when they pretend to be stupid about housework.

THE GUY SPEAKS: *"I'm just a little tired of this talk about how men don't understand women. First of all, we'd like to. We really would. It would be good for us! But maybe women could help a little by not being so complicated. No, it's not even that. Most guys have jobs where we have to figure out complicated stuff. It's just that a lot of women I get involved with, it really seems they try to seem as complicated as they can, and then they crap all over me for not figuring it out. I guess all I'm asking is that they try a little not to be so damned confusing."*

It's true that women can be pretty complicated sometimes. But I still think we should stop letting men off the hook. I admire the attitude of one of the women I talked to. Referring to guys she dates who suddenly stop calling her for a few days, Hazel, 29, coolly summed it up as "poor poon management!" Gross, but right on target! Maybe if men thought of us as a management problem, they'd be more diligent in boning up on the subject.

For some women the Holy Grail is a guy who "gets" you. Okay, but you don't need Einstein. You just need a guy who's willing to listen when you talk about how you work and who shows he can learn from it. Let's say that when you get mad you like to be left alone. But your guy starts out saying, "What's wrong? We should talk about it," whenever you get upset. If you say, "The best thing to do when I'm angry is ignore me," and he does it, that's a good sign. It means he's not so full of his own view of things that he can't learn.

But if your best efforts to supply your guy with an owner's manual to you go nowhere, then he's really not a guy who cares about you. He just cares about some vision he has in his head about you, and he'll make you miserable.

If he takes responsibility like a grown-up, that's a good sign. But if he tends to find excuses for his problems and mistakes, he's a loser.

Any guy you're with is going to screw up. Hell, we all screw up. Now just close your eyes and imagine for a moment how irritating it's going to be to live with a guy who's always finding excuses, often by blaming someone or something else.

Let's say he's late meeting you after work. Okay, these things happen. But if he always says things like, "You wouldn't believe the traffic. And then there was this thing I had to take care of at work . . ." you'll just go nuts. You want a guy who says something like, "I'm really sorry I'm late. I screwed up. I hope you didn't feel stupid sitting here waiting for me."

Think about it for a moment. If he's an excuse finder, he'll always feel he can get away with anything. And he'll always feel you're a big, fat meanie for being upset about anything he does. Why are you making such a big deal about his driving away having left the baby on the roof of the car? "Don't you understand how much is on my mind these days?"

If you don't want to always be in the wrong, and you don't want to feel that your life is constantly flying out of control, dump the guy who's an excuse finder.

On the other hand, think of how safe you'll feel if your guy's an actual grown-up who knows how to take responsibility. Remember, safety is a dimension of chemistry, and the dimensions interact: when one dimension goes up, the others tend to go up, too. If he makes you feel safer, you'll find you're also respecting him more and having more fun and being more at ease with him and . . .

If he's kind, that's an incredibly good sign. If he's mean and selfish, run for the hills.

They did a study in Massachusetts of guys who get into more than their share of car accidents. What personality characteristic would you guess is most associated with these guys? I would have guessed they were aggressive, type A guys, and I would've been wrong.

No, in fact the guys who got into more than their share of accidents were the ones who went around feeling *entitled*. For example, when the light turned green the car in front of one guy didn't start moving. So this entitled guy veered on to the sidewalk and hit a pedestrian. Afterward he wasn't even remorseful. "It was my light," he said.

My light, my poker night, my right to have sex whenever I want, my right to keep my money secret from you—these are all signs of mean, selfish, entitled guys. In judging your guy on this character trait, don't cheat yourself—you can do a lot better. Don't let him off the hook because he works so hard or because you know he had a really tough childhood. Just ask yourself if you could say the following statement: "I know my guy is warm, kind, and generous because he acts that way toward me almost all the time, and when he sees that something's really important to me, he really tries to make sure he comes through for me." If you couldn't say this, then that's a bad sign.

When the dog she loved since childhood got really sick and suddenly needed to be put to sleep, one woman called her boyfriend to be with her. He said, "Listen, I just teed off on the third hole. I'll be home as soon as I finish the course." This guy flunks. A guy who acts entitled is not entitled to you.

Kind guys—good. Mean guys—bad. It's really that simple. Or is it?

A kind guy who's weak does you no good. Maybe he's just kind because he's afraid of you. What you're really looking for is a strong, solid, tough guy who's also kind. I don't mean beat-'em-up tough. I mean self-reliant and persistent and resilient. When a guy like that is kind, you know you have something worth holding on to.

As for mean and selfish, you have to be careful here. Guys sometimes get so focused on work, so self-absorbed, that they can seem mean and selfish. On the one hand, you can't let his being busy and self-absorbed be an excuse for his being mean and selfish. What do you care *why* he acts that way? If he's crappy toward you, he's crappy toward you.

On the other hand, his acting mean and selfish might *only* come from his being busy and self-absorbed, and not at all from who he really is deep down. So the problem isn't with who he is. The problem is that a basically decent, sweet guy needs a big old wake-up call. You've got to say something to him like, "Look, I know you get so caught up in what you're doing. But that's absolutely no excuse for being selfish or acting mean. I'm a real person here and you've got to wake up to how I might be feeling."

If your guy responds to a wake-up call like this, then you're probably okay. Just ask yourself if you basically feel safe with him. That's your ultimate check. If he doesn't respond or if you don't feel safe, then you can't make excuses. He's going to be mean to you, and that tells you things just can't work.

If your guy knows how to behave with you, with your friends and family, and in the kinds of places you like to hang out, that's a good sign. But if he keeps behaving inappropriately, then it's appropriate for you to dump him.

Repeat after me: inappropriate isn't cute. This is serious. Guys who behave inappropriately either are losers or are very troubled. You need to stay away from them.

What do I mean by behaving inappropriately?

It's a kind of deep, weird cluelessness. Let's say you're about to make love and he makes some dumb comment about how you've put on weight and are looking "pouchy." It's bad enough that this hurts. But it's even worse that a guy would be so incredibly stupid as to make a woman feel fat, self-conscious, and unhappy at the very moment he's wanting to make love to her. *That's* inappropriate.

Let's say you're hanging out with friends and your guy keeps trying to dominate the conversation. Or he keeps talking about himself. Or he takes casual comments way too personally and gets offended. One way or another, he makes you and your friends feel uncomfortable. *That's* inappropriate.

Maybe he madly flirts with your sister. Maybe he gets into

big fights with salesclerks. Maybe he has oddball opinions that freak people out. Strange, long silences, maybe. *All* this is inappropriate.

This has nothing to do with whether he is somehow different. Different is fine. If he's more exuberant or quieter than people in your family, so what? The key is that he makes you feel uncomfortable not rarely, but remarkably often. That's where you draw the line.

Don't think you can coach a guy who behaves inappropriately. We're not talking about simple ignorance. Let's say your family's Jewish and he was raised as a Christian in an area where there weren't any Jews. He might need some pointers about how to behave with your family. That's fine. No one's born knowing how to behave in contexts different from what they're used to.

But if he behaves inappropriately in places where you would expect the average person to have his act together, how can your coaching help? Shouldn't his years of adulthood have already taught him how to behave? There's something missing here, and it's not your coaching.

If he's there for you when you need him, that's a good sign. But if he's lazy, he's a loser.

A lot of us get confused here. Few guys are so lazy that, like Homer Simpson, it's a big deal for them to go to work. If you get involved with a guy like that, well, you're Marge Simpson. Do you want to be Marge Simpson?

But going to work and doing his job is not enough to qualify him for not-being-lazy status. A lot of guys are *closet* lazybones. They manage to bring home a paycheck, but that's it. They'll work for money, but they won't work for you. And you'll know this is true because of how you feel—you'll just feel that he's not there for you when you need him, the way you need him.

You can't make excuses for him. The most insidious excuse is, "Well, he works so hard. . . ." Really? He works so hard he can't make love to you? He works so hard he can't take out the garbage without your reminding him? He works so hard he never wants to do anything you want to do? He works so hard he can't listen to you? *Come on!* What you've really got on your hands is a lazy guy with the excuse of a semidemanding job. He may bring home the bacon, but he won't be bringing home your bacon.

If he accepts you the way you are, that's a good sign. But if he goes on a drive to change you, he could turn into your worst nightmare.

Here's a pattern lots of women have reported to me. And I've also seen this in my work all too often. A woman gets involved with a guy. There's a lot of passion early on, a kind of counterfeit chemistry based on their not knowing each other well. The woman gets hooked big time. She's never experienced passion and intimacy like this. It's almost like a kind of addiction—she freaks out if she can't get her daily fix of him.

Then the guy senses his power, and his inner Svengali comes out. He turns into a control freak. Of course it's all framed as his being "helpful" at first. "I just want you to be the best *you*, because I know how great you can be."

This is intoxicating. It seems like praise. But it's control masquerading as praise. Invariably his criticism and dissatisfaction mounts. She starts wondering why there are suddenly so many things wrong with her. She tries to change, but of course it's hard. Impatient, he distances himself from her, using her addiction to him as a way of gaining more control over her.

You know you're in a relationship like this when you feel worse about yourself than you have in a long time. These are relationships where you break up and come back together over and over. You're so focused on what's wrong with you that it's hard to think there's anything wrong with the guy.

You're in big danger. Your focus on what's wrong with you and what's right with him is blinding you to the fact that you've signed up for a course in misery if you stay with him. It's your blindness that's putting you in danger. To make matters worse, it's hard for you not to believe him. Many of the things he criticizes about you have a grain of truth. Maybe you *would* look better if you lost ten pounds. Maybe you *do* talk too much.

But the man you were meant to be with is not going to make you feel the way this guy does. The man you were meant to be with is going to make you feel that you're fine just the way you are. You don't deserve anything less.

Because Svengali has put you under his spell, you're going to need help to get out from under. You're going to need a breakup buddy, a friend who keeps reminding you how bad this relationship is for you. In the end, you'll be grateful to this pal for the rest of your life.

THE GUY SPEAKS: *"Hey, I'll tell you what. I'll stop trying to change you. You stop trying to change me. I know I'll have found that great woman when neither of us is trying to change the other."*

GUYS YOU MIGHT THINK ARE LOSERS BUT AREN'T

One of the great things about focusing on chemistry is that it becomes so much more likely that you'll find buried treasure— a guy who will make you very happy that you might otherwise have overlooked or dismissed.

Helen, 36, was one of the many women I talked to who felt

she had real buried treasure in her past—she'd had all the five dimensions of great chemistry with Gary, but she'd let him get away. The thing is, Gary wasn't all that spectacular on the surface. He was shy, not outstandingly successful (although his job as an accountant was nothing to be ashamed of), and he wasn't as arty or crunchy-granola as Helen was. If he'd been offered up by an online dating service, Helen would have passed. But they lived in the same building, became friends, and grew to really care about each other. And a real passion developed between them over time.

Helen moved out of that building and suddenly Gary was a half-hour drive away. She found herself saying things like, "He's not my type" and "He's not as successful as I hoped" and "He's too quiet." A couple of years later, Helen realized that she'd been too young to appreciate the true value of what she'd found with Gary. He was real buried treasure, but she passed him over and later married a guy she could brag about but who made her miserable.

What if your guy is real buried treasure? Here are some things women say about guys who are perfectly fine but who we mistakenly overlook.

"He's not my type." "Not my type" too often means that you have preconceptions about who will make you happy. But so many women have ended up in great marriages with guys they were sure weren't their type.

Looking past "not my type" is important on every level. We're so glib about who's not our type. "I don't date businessmen. They're always so boring." "He rides a motorcycle—he must be scummy and stupid." "He's too blond!" "He's two years younger than me. No!"

You just have to keep telling yourself that nothing trumps chemistry. Let's say you have strong political convictions and never imagined that you could be with a guy who didn't share your convictions. But then it soon becomes clear that he's not into politics at all. Not your type? Maybe. But check out your chemistry. If you respect each other, if you feel at ease with each other, if you have fun with each other, then who cares about your lack of political compatibility.

Your guy's not being "your type" only matters if it affects your chemistry.

"He's not as successful as I'd hoped." Many of us growing up form a very strong picture of the kind of guy we'll marry. He'll definitely be someone special, we think. Did you see that *Seinfeld* episode where Elaine can't handle being with a guy who's a podiatrist? He just didn't reach Elaine's preordained level of success. A version of this was a woman I knew who wouldn't go out with guys who hadn't graduated from highly selective colleges.

But, again, you have to go back to your chemistry. If all five dimensions of chemistry are strong, then you should commit. If his not living up to your preordained standard of success still bothers you, then what you're really saying is that you're more interested in bragging rights than a real relationship.

"He's too shy." In the movies, shy guys are endearing, like Hugh Grant in *Four Weddings and a Funeral*. In real life, they're usually not as good-looking, and so they're usually overlooked. And we go along with this. Maybe he really isn't very special if he's so shy, we think.

One of the secrets of women who've found great shy guys is that they have private relationships with these guys. The guy they know when it's just the two of them is their special secret. Talk about buried treasure! No one sees or can imagine the great chemistry they have. If this is true for you, what do you care what other people think?

"He's not all that good-looking." Uh-oh. You were hoping for Brad Pitt. Now you find you're dating SpongeBob SquarePants. Do you bail? It depends. You have to be honest with yourself. If the point was to be able to show him off to your girlfriends, the fact that he's not so good-looking shouldn't matter as long as the two of you have great chemistry. His looks matter only in two cases:

1. His looks bother you. For example, his big old beer belly makes you uncomfortable. Wherever you go, you notice it and you're embarrassed.
2. His looks affect your sexual chemistry. Maybe he's a handsome guy but his bad skin makes you reluctant to make love with him. You don't want it to creep you out, but it does.

As long as his looks don't really bother you or affect your sexual chemistry, then don't let them get in the way of your having a relationship with a guy if you have great chemistry with him.

Bottom line

The guys who are keepers and the guys who are losers may not be who you think they are at first. Make sure you see your guy for who he really is. And if something's off, it's a no go. There are too many great guys out there, and the women who get the great guys are the ones who identify the losers the fastest and then move on.

"Can I Trust Him?"

As they were being tossed out of the Garden of Eden, Eve was doing the fast angry-woman walk. Adam ran to catch up to her. "Why are you angry?" he said lamely, grabbing her arm to stop her. She yanked her arm out of his hand and said, "You told me you were in tight with the Big Guy. You told me you owned this place. You told me you would take care of me. Now look at us. How can I ever trust you again?"

There you have it—one of the biggest reasons there's no chemistry in a relationship, because, after all, no trust, no safety, no chemistry. And so it's been from the beginning of time. The idea that too often you can't trust men is something we know in our bones. Starting from the day you and I went through puberty and developed a woman's body, some little middle-school guy taught us that some guys would say anything to get under our tops and into our pants. Then we learned that some guys would say anything to get out of having to commit. And then they'd lie, lie, lie to explain what they did with their money or how they spent their time when we weren't around.

I'm not saying all men are like this. I'm not saying any man is always like this. Listen, I like men. I'm just saying that this is the typical woman's experience of too many men.

And we have the *most* trouble trusting men when we're caught up in a developing relationship. In fact, no issue comes up more often for women in developing relationships than trust. When I asked women I interviewed what areas they needed help in, this was their number one concern: "I want to be able to trust this guy, but I don't know how." It's not that they *knew* the guy was untrustworthy. They were pretty sure he was mostly a good guy. But there were big question marks and they didn't know how to get answers.

THE GUY SPEAKS: *"I get really mixed feelings when I hear a woman talk about how hard it is to trust guys. I want to say, you should see some of the stuff some of the women I've been with have pulled. Or tried to pull. And I want to say this about me—I'm a really nice guy. Some women think I'm too nice, which is a whole other thing. But honestly, I hear stories, stuff guys have told me about stuff they've done, and I think about some things I've done, and I think about how I'd feel if some of these women were my sister. It kills me to say this, but I wish women were more careful about the guys they got involved with."*

TRUST BY STAGES

The "Can I trust you?" issue often comes up on the first date. A number of women told me that they and their friends found that every man you meet from an online dating site lies about his height. "Five-ten," they said, "is code for five-six." I guess five-six would mean the guy's really a peanut. So you can find trust issues flooding you the minute the guy stands up to his full "height" to utter whatever stupid opening line he's been re-hearsing for the last three days.

Then as you sit there on the first date, your mistrust deepens. Hmmm, you think, this guy looks older and seedier than he did when I saw his picture online. Now he's telling me how he's this big-shot "freelance financial adviser." What does that mean?

Maybe he is. But maybe he's just unemployed. How can I know for sure? Good question. There are women who never really learn the full truth about their guy's money or career, even long after they're married. And the same for all the other areas where trust comes up.

It can even be hard to trust really honest guys. There are some guys who reek of honesty. They'll lay it on the line about all their flaws, but then they'll lay it on the line about all *your* flaws. So even if you can trust them to tell the truth, you don't know if you can trust them to be nice to you.

It's important that you trust your own lack of trust. Don't dismiss it. Kristen, 39, had been on two dates with Dan. He was supposed to be pretty well off, but she found he was promising her lots of things that sounded fishy. He was going to take her out for a day on his friend's yacht. He was going to let her use a friend's cabin in the Berkshires. He had a friend in the travel business who could get her cut-rate airfares.

There's nothing wrong with a guy being openhearted and generous. But why all these promises? Didn't Dan have any stuff of his own he could offer? And who were all these "friends" who could do all these things? Kristen smelled a rat. But she didn't trust her own lack of trust. She told me, "I'd been burned so many times and I'd gotten so mistrustful that I was just sick of being mistrustful." Amazing, isn't it? Sometimes we can actually have so little trust that it exhausts us to the point where we forget to be careful at all. (Of course Dan turned out to be an exaggerator and a con man.)

And trust issues can extend right through the wedding day itself. Elizabeth, 36, said, "We had this lovely evening reception. After the dinner and the toasts, Frank was supposed to come up to my room and help me out of my dress. *We'd talked about that.* It was going to be so romantic. I waited and waited. Finally my mother had to help me out of it. It was so humiliating. I went downstairs to look for him. There he was on a lounge chair with his buddies, drinking and smoking a cigar. He said he was waiting for me to call him when I was ready, but really *he'd forgotten all about me.*" You won't be surprised to hear that they divorced later.

But then how do you trust the next guy when you know things can go so very wrong even at the last minute?

THE NEED TO TRUST

If you're in a developing relationship, you're going to be in trouble unless you can find a way to *know* whether you can trust your guy. If you can't find a way, you'll never be able to read the chemistry between the two of you. There will always be a part of you that thinks you can't trust him. This will cause you to close off part of your feelings—the most vulnerable part of you. But it's precisely this tender self, this loving, hopeful, open self, that does the work of reading the chemistry. And that's in part because the more loving and open you are, the more you get to see what he's really like.

You see why you've got to know if you can trust him or not. Plus, hell is living on a bed of nails of suspicion. In a situation like that, even neutral information—"Honey, I'm going to be late. I'm stuck in traffic"—can feel like a stab in the heart. Yeah, right, you think.

There are plenty of trustworthy guys. So most of us can save a lot of heartache and move on much faster to a good relationship if we dump the guy who shows he's just not reliable. If you can't trust him, you've not found a home for your heart. Better homes await you.

When Barbara, 33, met Eric, she trusted him because she felt he accepted her more than any guy since her first boyfriend in high school. Now let's see how things turned out.

Very pretty and curvy, Barbara dressed in a funky way and

was just a little on the plump side. Guys turned their heads to look at her when she walked down the street. She was quirky, too. Her small graphics design business was doing well, but she was completely disorganized. She fluttered and fumbled through life but she was so sweet and funny that she made it okay.

It was easy for Barbara to meet guys, and they seemed to like her, but they also seemed to have trouble staying interested in her, and she could never figure out why. When she was 31, Barbara was starting to get discouraged.

Then she met Eric, who did something boring in the financial district. For Barbara the great thing about Eric was that he seemed to totally accept and understand her. Over and over he gave Barbara the message that she was perfect just the way she was. Not skinny enough? "You have a perfect voluptuous woman's body." Too insecure and ditzy? "You're the cutest woman I've ever known. You just make me want to take care of you." "Really?" Barbara said, tears of relief frosting her eyelashes. "Forever," Eric said, kissing her tears away.

Things changed after Barbara moved into Eric's apartment. From the moment she walked in carrying a box of her belongings, Barbara had this intuition, "Now he's got me." She suddenly wondered if she could trust how nice he'd been. She tried to dismiss that thought but it stayed with her.

Her intuition was accurate. Their difficulties started with Eric making friendly, helpful suggestions about how Barbara could improve herself. "You know, if you just made to-do lists, you wouldn't be so scattered." Plus there were his ever-so-slightly-irritated pointers about how he liked things in *his* apartment: "If you get home before me, you've got to take the dog out for a walk right away. Look what happens if you wait," Eric said pointing to a pile of dog poop. This was reasonable, but the patronizing tone got to her.

Barbara tried to be accommodating, but more and more she

found herself pushing back when he said things like this. After all, hadn't Eric said he liked her feisty independence? Evidently not as much as she'd thought.

Their battles escalated. It was tough for Barbara to feel rejected. But even worse was the sense that Eric had been so accepting. Who was this new Eric? It was very confusing. Barbara wanted her old Eric back. She didn't know if she could trust this new version, or her perceptions of him.

She felt she had to find out what she could trust. And so, like tons of women in developing relationships, Barbara was hooked trying to figure out what was real.

That's the problem when you start having trouble trusting a guy. It's almost as if you have to hang around to see how it's going to turn out. Who will the real Eric be? Barbara had to know the answers to her questions, the way you might hang around watching a really boring crime show because you got hooked at the beginning and you've got to see who done it.

She also hung around because she desperately *wanted* to trust him. That's a deep need for most of us. Men can seem alien enough. But if you get to the point where it's hard to trust men, where every guy has to prove how trustworthy he is to you standing there with your arms folded and a suspicious look on your face, then it's just exhausting and demoralizing. It makes you feel, Why bother?

Here are the areas where we have the most trouble trusting our guys: Does he want to be in a committed relationship? Is he a good guy? When he tells you about the kind of guy he is— energetic, nature loving, generous, ambitious, hardworking, social, family oriented—is he lying or deceiving himself? Has he seriously misrepresented how much baggage he's bringing into the relationship—problems with his ex, old emotional wounds, financial and health problems, demands his parents or his kids make on him? Has he lied about the kind of job he really has or about how much money he's got?

Sounds tough, doesn't it? But I'm very optimistic about our ability to deal with the issue of trust. After all, you're probably not in the grips of some evil genius.

Nine times out of ten, your problem is that you're unwilling to see who your guy really is, or you don't know what to look for. Open your eyes and call it like it is—not how you wish it was.

You *can* figure out if it makes sense to trust your guy. You can learn to see the real guy. You can learn to read the signs that provide important clues about how much you can trust him. And I'll show you how.

WHAT NOT TO DO

If you want to stop being bamboozled by guys, here's what *not* to do.

Don't operate under the puppy-dog theory. We don't do this deliberately, of course. But we do it. We figure that if a guy started out cute, he must be okay. Once he makes the cut, we make excuses for him. That's what Barbara was doing with Eric. He'd been so accepting at first—that's when he earned his cute-puppy-dog credentials. So when he changed radically, Barbara acted as if the impatient, intolerant guy she'd moved in with was less real than the cute guy who'd tried to win her.

Barbara just couldn't make sense of Eric's new behavior. And if it didn't make sense, Barbara thought, it couldn't be real. "Surely this is not my sweet Eric." It's easy for us to be blind to what doesn't make sense. But there's actually good news here.

Here's how it works. Every time a woman makes an excuse for a guy, she starts with positive experiences she's had with him. He has puppy-dog eyes! He's told me he loves me!

We've had great sex! We've spent a lot of time together! This creates a fixed idea in her mind of who the guy is, which blinds her to something that shouldn't be so hard to see. It's almost as if we believe, "If I've kissed the frog, how can he not turn into a prince?"

And don't start blaming yourself. The guy you're having trouble trusting today is a guy you let yourself trust yesterday. So even though he's betrayed your trust, you do what most women do. You turn the searchlight on yourself. Suddenly it's not so much that the guy betrayed you but that you let yourself be misled. And soon this sets up a state of radical self-mistrust. You become one of those women who say, "I'm not good at picking men."

But that's probably not true. I'll bet you could be great at picking men. If you open your eyes, you have everything you need to see clearly.

As I've said, don't close your eyes to what's real. If you let yourself see who your guy really is, you probably won't get bamboozled.

So what do you look for when you're trying to decide if you can trust him?

WHAT TO LOOK FOR

Smart women care very much about protecting their ability to be hopeful and nurturing. They understand that they'll lose this ability if they keep hooking up with guys who betray them. *They have to be tough so they can stay soft.*

So here's how these smart women operate. They use certain common-sense procedures for checking out their guys just the way they'd check out a guy they were hiring to do a job in their house. And to employ each procedure, they just have to look and see.

Can I Trust My Guy?
Step 1: Ask yourself, "Does he have a good track record? Is who he seems to be consistent with who he has been?" The past is a great predictor of the future.

> **If your guy has a good track record, you can trust him.**
> **Bad track record? Bad guy.**

You have to look at his track record in every part of his life that's important to you. His work and financial history. His relationships with friends and family.

Let's look at what it means to do this by focusing on his romantic history. Did he cheat on his exes? Abuse them? Dump them for no good reason? Stay loyal? This means finding out both from him and maybe from his friends and family how those relationships really ended.

It's a good sign if he hung in there in his previous relationships and tried to make them work. It's a good sign if he learned things from what went wrong in his relationships and if he can tell you what he learned and if it makes sense to you.

It's a bad sign if he cheated on his exes. It's a bad sign if they dumped him because he was lying. It's a bad sign if they found out he was just a bag of empty promises.

Now here's an important issue, because it comes up a lot. Does one of these bad signs become a good sign if he claims he's learned his lesson? *No.* His claim is not enough. Nor are his tears, or his heartfelt protestations while he's pounding the cushions on your couch—none of that is enough.

Here's what you do have in this case. You have both a bad sign (bad track record) and a good sign (he claims he's learned his lesson). They don't average out to a neutral sign. The bad sign stays, fully bad: he *is* the kind of guy who would do that.

Now maybe he's also the kind of guy who would do that only once. Could be. It sure helps to know that he says he's learned his lesson and never wants to destroy a good relationship by being an idiot again.

But the bad sign is still there. Here are some ways you can determine how bad this bad sign is.

Is there a pattern of bad behavior? Using the issue of cheating as an example, has he cheated on all his exes, or only one time in all his previous relationships? If he's cheated on all his exes, well, come on—that's a really bad sign. If he's cheated only once, only one single time—then the bad sign may not be quite so bad.

Is the bad behavior part of his personality? Do you see in him a pattern of cheating in other areas of life—cheating on his bosses, making promises he doesn't keep, cheating on the golf course or at cards? The thing is that cheaters cheat. It's a personality trait, and it rarely confines itself to a few areas of a person's life. It's a very bad sign if you see a pattern of cheating.

You should always look for patterns and believe the patterns you see.

Now what do you do if it turns out your guy has a suspicious track record? I'll lay it out for you. If he has a really bad track record—definitely worse than that of other guys you've gone out with, definitely the kind of track record that would make you want to give your sister a wake-up smack if you found out she was dating a guy like this—well, you tell me. On what planet is it smart to stay in this relationship? The planet where all the women walk around with a KICK ME sign on their backs? Would you buy a used car if the salesman said, "It's had a lot of problems in the past, but hopefully they've gone away"? Only if you came from the Kick Me planet.

I've talked about how love makes us stupid. Here's where we see that at its worst. A woman gets involved with a guy with a bad track record but he sucks her in with puppy-dog eyes, passionate promises that he'll change, declarations of eternal love, and then something else that he dangles in front of her. It could be anything. A dazzling smile. A glamorous lifestyle. A boat. This is when we start to make excuses. We make up stories about how he's changed or about how the bad stuff in his track record really wasn't so bad. In other words, we believe what we want to believe because it's more romantic that way.

But his track record is the best way you can tell if you can trust him. Sometimes people change, but usually people are tomorrow the way they were yesterday. If you don't see the change, believe the track record.

A person is who he is, not who he says he's going to be. Make sure you commit to him for the person he is right now, based on what you know about how he's been in the past.

If you're pleasantly surprised as the years go by, hey, that's great. The key is to set yourself up for pleasant surprises. If you decide to be with someone based on who you think he might become, you're setting yourself up for unpleasant surprises.

When you see an inconsistency with a guy, go with what makes sense, not with what you want to believe. Real inconsistencies are a bad sign.

For example, if he says he has completely broken off relations with his ex, well, in and of itself that may very well be true. But if you know their story and sense that things never really ended with them, there's an inconsistency there.

If he claims to be a serious, hardworking guy but he has only dirtball, go-nowhere friends, there's an inconsistency there.

If you're looking for real love that will last, then don't believe the best *or* the worst about him. Believe the *truth* about him. And it's by looking for inconsistencies that you'll discover the truth.

Now suppose his track record isn't *so* bad. He has screwed up, but not terribly. Or suppose you just don't know how to evaluate his track record. Or suppose you're both in your twenties and he doesn't have much of a track record.

Just ask yourself how safe you feel with him. This is a time when feelings are very important, especially the feelings that come up at those times when you're lying awake in the middle of the night and worries are rolling around in your head.

If you just plain old don't feel safe, that's a bad sign. Don't overthink it. Just leave. Don't ever stay with a guy with whom you don't feel safe.

If you think it's hard to leave now, just think how much harder it will be when you have kids or a house together. The most important thing is not wasting time with a guy who will mess you up.

Step 2: Pay attention to whether he complains about his exes.

If he complains a lot about previous relationships, that shows he's probably a demanding, hard-to-satisfy guy. Complaints also could indicate that he's someone who blames others, not himself. Watch out. This is a bad sign.

A guy who complains about his exes can soon end up your judge and jury. And if he complains a lot about his exes, it may also be that he's really bad at choosing women who can make him happy over the long haul. What if you're a mistake for him, too?

Here's how to draw the line. When you ask him about a previous relationship, it makes total sense that he'd talk about the problems there. He might very well have one or two specific complaints about that ex. Fine. This is what you asked him about.

But if all he does is complain about all his exes, or if every time you ask he gives you long lists of complaints, say bye-bye to him. He's not a guy who likes women or who has good judgment about women. He's what I call a hypothetical heterosexual— he's attracted to women in theory, but he just doesn't like us when he gets us.

Step 3: See how open your guy is.

> **One of the best things you can do to see if you can trust a guy is check out how vulnerable and open he is. There's one question you need to ask yourself: "Does he give me a true and complete picture of himself?"** *Yes* **is a good sign.** *No* **is a bad sign.**

Of course everyone tries to put the best light on things. But guys you can trust show you their warts and worries. *This makes you safe.* Let's say you've recently gotten involved with a guy whose ex hurt him badly. She was the one who ended things. He's only recently been able to let her go. Now, are you safer if he tells you about his occasional feelings for her or if he hides them? Are you safer if he tells you that he broke down and called her or if he hides that from you?

Sure, you wish he didn't call her or have feelings for her. But that's not the point. The point is that right now these are facts. And if you don't know them, then you've got a guy in your life who's dealing with this all by himself, and who knows where he'll go with it. The whole thing could blow up in your face, badly. You won't know how to evaluate whether he's really over his ex until you've gotten deeper and deeper into your developing relationship with him. You could spend months or even years being his emotional flotation device until, who knows, he maybe patches things up with her. Now that's a nightmare.

The way to get openness and vulnerability is, first of all, to expect it. Don't let some Mars/Venus bullshit blind you to the fact that he should be open and that he can be open. I know countless testosterone-packed guys who don't have the slightest problem being vulnerable. If you're getting involved with a guy and you find that he just doesn't open up after a few dates, make him your ex immediately.

The other thing you need to do is reward your guy when he's open with you. That's surprisingly hard for some of us. We want to feel safe, but we like strong guys, and if we're really honest, we don't want to give up our monopoly on emotions. Plus "being open" is, if I'm going to be open with you, really often code for "telling you stuff you won't like hearing," and who wants to encourage that?

Here's your best move. Let's say your guy says something that shows he's being vulnerable. You know that's what it is because it makes you feel uneasy or unhappy. It doesn't take any vulnerability on his part to say something that makes you happy. By being so open he's just handed you a lifeline; he's showing you that he can be trusted. So your move always has to be, "I'm so glad you told me that." Then talk to him about what he said. Have a conversation. No harangue. No third degree. No emotional fireworks. No putting him under the microscope. You have one goal: to make him feel, "Wow, I can tell her anything."

By the way, if he was having doubts about you, this will go far toward easing them. This is one of those dirty little secrets about men I wish more of us knew.

Men love women who are easy to talk to. After all, ease is the first of the five dimensions of chemistry. If you've wondered why a guy has dropped you, it's possible that he didn't find you easy to talk to. Lots of us are good listeners but bad commenters on what we've heard. And it's our comments that stop the guys from talking.

In particular, you have to watch your tendency to judge or overanalyze what he says when he's opening up. You need to trust your guy. You can do that only if he's open. Don't do anything to jeopardize that. Nothing's more important.

Step 4: Find out if he lies. A lot of guys will find you so desirable that they will say anything to get you. You might find this hard to believe (or if you're conceited, you might find it easy to believe!). They will, in other words, lie. They'll lie about how much money they have. They'll lie about their success. Whatever they think will impress you, they'll lie about it.

Here's one of my favorite lie stories. On her second date with Tim, Heidi, 31, was complaining about her ex. What an uptight bore he was. Tim asked for examples. Heidi found herself mentioning that her ex was lazy and selfish in bed. Tim recoiled in horror that any guy could possibly be that way with someone as lovely as her. Tim sensed his moment. He said, "If you were with me, I'd give you hours of oral sex every day. I love doing that. And I'm sure I'd love doing that with you."

Heidi's eyes got big as saucers. She was too embarrassed to say anything—after all, this was only their second date—but she was deeply impressed. She figured Tim was exaggerating. But still. Even if she cut his claim in half—hours of oral sex every other day? A half an hour every day?—it sounded pretty good to her.

But it was just a line. Tim had sensed an opening and he went for it. The real truth? Tim was willing occasionally to give her oral sex, but he got tired easily. At least Heidi's ex hadn't teased her.

So how do you deal with this kind of thing, where a guy says something to impress you? Your attitude has to be "I'll believe it when I see it."

You shouldn't assume there's any truth in what he's saying when he makes big claims. Be grateful for the fact that he likes you enough to try to impress you, but leave it at that. You don't have to say anything to

him about your suspicions, but keep your eye out for evidence.

Give him a chance to prove his claim. If he says he knows famous people, for example, fine. But don't move any further in this developing relationship than you have already until he actually produces some of these people. And the more his claim seems too good to be true or at odds with what you see, the more skeptical you have to be. There really aren't a lot of eccentric millionaires who just happen to prefer living in rundown apartments. Guys who work in music stores probably aren't close friends with Diddy.

Just remember to watch out for guys you catch working at impressing you.

A SPECIAL SECRET FOR FIGURING OUT IF YOU CAN TRUST YOUR GUY

Lynn, 43, said, "The only way you can know for sure that you can trust a guy you're with is if he treats you the same way when he becomes rich and successful."

I understand what she was getting at. It's only when a guy is rich and successful that he can do whatever he wants. More women will be attracted to him. The cost of ending things with you won't matter so much to him. So if a guy in *that* position continues to treat you right, you know it's real and you know you're safe.

But this is pretty useless advice. Most guys don't become so rich and successful that they can do whatever they want. And even if they do, you can wait a long time for them to get there.

I've got much better advice. Instead of waiting for him to get to the place where he can do whatever he wants, why don't *you* start being freer to be *yourself* now. It's a much faster, much easier route to being able to trust him. Just let it all hang out, as early as possible, as if *you* were so rich and successful yourself that you just didn't care what he thought of you. Yes, I know—you do care. But what good does it do you? All it does is put you on your best behavior, and all *this* does is set up the situation where you have no idea how he'll react when he sees the real you.

So be the real you *now*. See how he reacts *now*. Okay, maybe when you let yourself show your moodiness he'll freak out and take a hike. That hurts, but it's actually really good that you found this out now. Your guy was a Hidden Dud. He couldn't handle you being you, so he quit before you could fire him.

But suppose you show yourself as you really are and discover that he hangs in there and stays interested. In a world where trust is hard to come by, that's pure gold.

Bottom line

Don't worry so much about trusting your guy. Be more concerned about seeing him for who he really is, and accepting what you see. And understand that you're not seeing him for who he really is unless you've shown yourself for who you really are.

"How Does He *Really* Feel About Me?"

L ily, 29, a woman born in China but living in New York for the past ten years, said about the men she'd been dating, "They are nice, so sweet and nice until women try to discuss where we are at. Then they freak out, then their behavior changes and they become as cold as ice. Some men just want to have sex, that's the reason. Some men I was dating have a serious issue being in relationships. Then why do they ask women out? Why do they keep seeing women? They know they will hurt women sooner or later. But they can't stop seeing women. That's the reality. Work on your own issues first and see women when you overcome them!"

Lily's right, of course. It's too bad we can't issue a no-dating-me-unless-you're-serious directive, enforceable by law. But we can't. That leaves us trying to figure out what it means when guys do things.

A while back, it seems we thought that when a guy acted uninterested, he was secretly longing for us. He just couldn't express it. "I know he wants me." Then along came an episode of *Sex and the City* and the pendulum shifted. Suddenly the idea was that if a guy's into you, he'll be all over your ass. So if he's not getting the job done, he must not be into you. "I know he doesn't want me."

He loves me. He loves me not. *Pant. Pant. Pant.* Sorry, but I'm out of breath keeping up with the pendulum going back and forth. It's time we applied a little common sense. And we need to get clear about this because if you make a mistake here, it can be huge.

I'm a case in point.

"DON'T CALL ME, I'LL CALL YOU."

When I met my husband, there was an immediate connection. We had ten days of magical chemistry. Then he casually mentioned, "Oh, by the way, this girl I was seeing is coming back from Mexico in a month. Of course she's not really my girlfriend anymore now that I've met you, but I'm going to have to break up with her when she gets back."

I had trouble feeling safe anyway, so this freaked me out. Why hadn't he told me about this sooner? There's no way I'd be involved with a guy who was involved with someone else. There's no way I'd be involved with a guy who wasn't absolutely open and honest from the beginning.

I tried to kick him out, but unfortunately I happened to be in his apartment when he told me. So I did this whole angry walking-out scene. My exit line was, "Don't call me. I'll call you." [Sound of door slamming.]

A month went by. I couldn't believe it. *He didn't call me.* It didn't make sense. Yeah, I knew what I'd said. But when had a guy ever taken me literally before? Particularly when it came to something he wanted? Wouldn't he at least try to get through to me? I was expecting he'd call me every day. He'd clearly been head over heels for me. And yet he wasn't calling me. Was he just not that into me?

It wasn't just idle curiosity. During that month apart I realized that those had been the best ten days of my life. He was very special, and I missed him and wanted him. Plus I wanted to know why the hell he wasn't calling.

So finally I caved and called him. Thank God, I could hear him nearly fainting with relief when he heard my voice. It turns out that he'd been in hell since I'd walked out on him. Absolute hell.

So why hadn't he called me? Because he wasn't all that into me?

No. It was because I'd said, "Don't call me. I'll call you." He'd listened to me and taken me literally! I now know that my husband is very tied to the literal meaning of words. He's not stupid. He's brilliant! But he's always been that way about everything. He just takes what you tell him literally.

Now if I'd assumed that he wasn't all that into me, my entire life would have been very different, and I can't imagine that it would have been better.

GETTING AT THE TRUE STORY

We need to stop the pendulum. It was very wrong for all of us to live in a fool's paradise where we created fantasy guys who we were sure really cared about us but didn't. But it's equally wrong to assume that there's this Standard Guy who operates in a certain way, otherwise he's just not that into you.

> THE GUY SPEAKS: *"I'm kind of mad about this idea that guys are really such simple, primitive, dumb creatures, that you can just sum us up. All I ask is, just because I like to watch football, don't think you know me. And you know what? If something about me confuses you, just ask. I'll tell you."*

There are all kinds of guys. Some suffer from their own sweet kind of cluelessness. Some are just marching to the beat of a different drummer.

Some are coming off an experience that you may not be fully aware of. Mark was just not getting physical with Deedee, 30.

She told me how weird it felt. There was a real emotional connection. But at all the times she was expecting him to make a move, he didn't. No passionate kisses, no reaching for her breasts, nothing. Was he gay? Did he just not find her desirable?

Finally, Deedee broke down and asked Mark what the hell was going on. At first Mark just said he was sorry, but he didn't really offer an explanation. Then Deedee pushed a little and it all came out. It seems that Mark had been involved with a predatory woman who'd used sex to hook him and then told him he was a lousy lover. Mark was lucky he could date at all!

And, by the way, Mark said he was so physically attracted to Deedee that it was driving him nuts.

When you assume, you make an *ASS* out of *U* and *ME*. Find out what's really going on when your guy does things that don't make sense to you.

That's the key. Getting information. Here are some tips:

Let's say that he just doesn't call you very often. There are two things you want. You want him to call more frequently. You want to know why he doesn't call so often.

Now your best move is to just ask for what you want and skip the explanations. You could say, for example, "Look, we're in a relationship, and I'd really like it if you called me more often, like every day." If he says, "Oh, okay," then you've saved yourself a lot of bickering. You're always better off asking for what you want than asking for an explanation. Talk to him in a reasonable way about how his always putting you off with stories about how busy he is makes you feel rejected. Is that what he's doing, trying to reject you? Maybe since your guy was recently appointed to the president's cabinet, he really really is so busy. See? Now you know.

But maybe he's full of it. Don't let his brilliant, heartfelt explanation distract you from the main point, which is getting your needs met. His explanation should help you work something out so you can go on to get your needs met. Don't settle for a guy who doesn't deliver the goods.

If you do need to understand why he's doing what he's doing, then understand this: the most likely reason your guy is going to have trouble telling you the truth is that he's afraid it's going to be a big hassle if he does so. He's afraid that every answer he gives is going to raise a dozen more questions. He's afraid that if he says one wrong thing, you're going to get upset. So you have to say something like, "Look, I'm not going to bust your chops over this or get into a big hassle with you. I just want to understand why you don't call me very often. Whatever you say is fine. I just want to know."

Now, it's fine if when he says something that you don't quite get you ask more questions. But you've got to make it clear that you're just looking for clarification. You're not looking for an excuse to play gotcha. And remember, the calmer you are, the more easily your guy will open up.

If you've made it as easy as humanly possible for him to talk to you about why, for example, he doesn't call you very often, and he still won't give you a straight story, then fine. Dump him. It's not about whether he's into you or not. It's that he's a guy who doesn't know how to treat you. You aren't into him.

FEELING HE LIKES YOU

Even if you can't make sense of everything your guy does, even if you can't get all your needs met (and none of us can), you still deserve, at a minimum, to know that your guy likes you. That's one of the payoffs from having good chemistry. Feeling liked is enormously important. Feeling loved can be very abstract. Feeling liked is something you know in your gut. It's not about words.

He doesn't like you if he keeps telling you how terrific you'd be if you made certain changes. He likes you if he genuinely enjoys you just the way you are.

He doesn't like you if he only wants to have sex with you. He likes you if he enjoys hanging out with you after you've made love.

He doesn't like you if he spends money on you. He likes you if he spends time with you.

He doesn't like you if he keeps telling you how pretty you are. He likes you if he likes the way you act.

Bottom line

Men aren't all the same. You can't make assumptions about what certain actions mean. So no guessing games. Do your best to find out why your guy is doing what he's doing. If his explanation makes sense, you've saved yourself from a pointless breakup. But explanations aren't the main thing. If he can't deliver the goods, you've got to throw him out on his ear.

"WHAT ABOUT OUR LIFESTYLE
DIFFERENCES?"

Alisha, 26, came to me recently and asked for help. "I met this guy, and oh my God, we have such good chemistry. Now here's what's confusing. We're at that point in our relationship where we're starting to talk about how we want to live, and I'm seeing that we have these differences. I'm not saying they're a big deal, but I know I want kids, and he has a kid from his previous marriage and kind of thinks that's that. Also, we both like living in the city but he also really likes living in the country and I'm not crazy about country living. What does this mean about whether we're right for each other?"

The question Alisha's really asking is, Does chemistry trump lifestyle differences or do lifestyle differences trump chemistry?

Let me answer this by telling you about two couples I worked with. We'll call them the Smiths and the Browns. The men both had kids in previous marriages. They felt they'd been there, done that. Now they just wanted to enjoy life without another kid in the picture. Both women were at least ten years younger than their men and very much wanted a child. As you can imagine, there was a lot of anger and frustration as they struggled with each other to get what they wanted. After all, you can't have half a baby.

So how do you think things turned out? Did both couples break up because they couldn't find a compromise?

Guess again. Here's how it played out. The Smiths had great chemistry in all five dimensions. You could just feel that they really clicked. The Browns were the opposite. Very little chemistry. They'd had what seemed like chemistry when they were first falling in love, but it was mostly sexual chemistry and they had it only when they were hanging out just the two of them. The slightest stress in their lives immediately canceled their chemistry, what little of it they had.

Although they came to me far apart on the baby issue, their good chemistry had a healing effect on the Smiths. Their closeness, ease, fun, affection, sense of safety, and respect enabled them to come to an amazing compromise. She accepted the fact that he'd paid his dues with his previous kid and was willing to take on total responsibility for caring for their new baby. That was it. They were both happy.

This might not work for everyone. Most of us need to feel that our guy will really pitch in when it comes to caring for the baby. But Mrs. Smith understood why her husband felt the way he did.

Of course, as I suspected, once the baby came, Mr. Smith changed his tune. He fell in love with the baby. It seems to be pretty much the rule that people who have good chemistry with each other have good chemistry with their kids.

But because the Browns had lousy chemistry, they couldn't come up with any solution at all. They just fought and grew more and more distant.

So here's how to think about the issue of lifestyle issues versus chemistry.

I've never seen a case where good chemistry didn't overcome lifestyle differences. And I've never seen a case where being in sync on lifestyle issues could overcome bad chemistry.

Now you might say, "But doesn't lifestyle matter at all?" Of course it matters. The closer together you are on lifestyle issues, the easier things will be. So if right now you're lucky enough to be involved with two men and you have great chemistry with both, then by all means go with the guy who likes to live the way you like to live. It's just so much gravy.

But that's not the kind of choice most of us face.

WHAT TO LOOK FOR

If you and your guy have great chemistry, you're all set. If it happens that you're not in sync on some lifestyle issues, that's too bad, but great chemistry's special, and it almost always gives you what you need to overcome those lifestyle differences. So, great chemistry? End of story.

If you and your guy have okay chemistry, then every bit of lifestyle conflict is going to make more and more of a difference. Be very suspicious about the viability of this relationship if there are important ways you're in conflict. I'm not talking about political opinions, for example. I'm talking about ways you don't mesh that have to do with how you actually live.

Here are the most important areas in which incompatibility will damage a relationship with mediocre chemistry. Check off each one that applies to you:

- Money: very different attitudes toward spending and saving.
                    This is true about me and my guy _____.
- Social life: one of you is very gregarious and the other's a loner.
                    This is true about me and my guy _____.
- Having kids: there's a big gap in how many kids each of you wants.
                    This is true about me and my guy _____.

- Childrearing: one of you is laid back; the other is very strict.

This is true about me and my guy _____.

- City or country: you want to live in very different kinds of places.

This is true about me and my guy _____.

- Ambition: one of you is very ambitious and is willing to make a lot of sacrifices to get ahead and the other just doesn't care about this.

This is true about me and my guy _____.

- Sex: there's a wide gap in how often the two of you want to make love.

This is true about me and my guy _____.

- Sleep: the gap between your sleep patterns is so great that generally you neither go to sleep together nor get up together.

This is true about me and my guy _____.

How many did you check off? Unless your chemistry is truly great, it's a very bad sign if you've checked off three or more of these important areas.

If you and your guy have poor chemistry, don't be confused by situations in which you have great compatibility. You're totally in agreement about how you like to live. You just don't like each other. Your lack of chemistry will inevitably create cracks in your relationship no matter how compatible you are.

Bottom line

Great chemistry? End of story. Chemistry trumps lifestyle differences.

ALL ABOUT YOU

"AM I EVEN *READY* FOR A RELATIONSHIP?"

There are many reasons why we might not be ready for a new relationship. For example, unless you're a kid, to fall in love means to fall in love *again*. And that means falling in love filled with the memory of how things went wrong in previous relationships. If those memories are troubling, we may not be ready for a new relationship. And one of the biggest ways we screw up our ability to read the chemistry in our developing relationship is that we're not ready for it in the first place.

If you have a stomachache after lunch, or you're really full, you're probably not ready to think about what you want for dinner yet. The same kind of thing happens with relationships.

Take Beth, 29: "This whole thing would be easier—deciding who's right for me—if I didn't have exes. But of course I do have exes and that's the problem. At the top of my list of things I want in a guy—and I know it's stupid—is I want him to not be like Joey, my asshole ex. He was sexy, but he was such a mean prick and he had a gambling problem.

"I can't get my ex out of my head. If I meet a new guy, my feelings are all tangled up with how he's like or not like my ex. The whole thing's such a mess. I'd love to just be with a guy and see him for who he is."

IF YOU'RE NOT READY,
YOU'RE NOT READY

You can want a relationship but if you're not ready, you're not ready, just the way you can want guests to visit but if you haven't cleaned your place and there's no food and nothing to drink, you're not ready. And not being ready takes a toll.

"I just don't know if this is the guy I want to spend the rest of my life with. I'm so scared I'll make another mistake. I'm not sure my poor little heart can take it," Tracy, 30, said to me. It's starting to bother her, the fact that it's taking her so long to find someone who's right for her. Shouldn't it be a lot easier? "People tell me I'm a good listener. Fun, easygoing, relaxed. Honest and loyal. Bubbly and upbeat. Not high maintenance! So why is it so hard?"

Tracy's last relationship had started out great. It's true that they both had tempers and they'd get into the occasional fight, but everything that should have been good was good. They were talking about getting married when suddenly Frank got offered a big job in New York.

Frank wanted to take it. He believed that if he took that job, in a few years they'd be set for life. Frank kept hammering away at the idea that Tracy would easily be able to find a job in New York. "And then you'll visit people on the West Coast all the time." But Frank just couldn't let it in that Tracy's work and family and friends were all in San Francisco. It wasn't about Tracy's finding a job. It was about Tracy's hating to leave her life. Plus she'd always hated the East Coast.

Things really soured when Frank started saying things like, "If you really loved me, you'd come with me." And Tracy would say things like, "If you really loved me, you'd understand how hard this is for me." In the end, Frank left and the relationship petered out. Tracy was heartbroken. For her, nothing had been resolved. It was like a death without a body. She still wanted Frank.

Before long Tracy started a new relationship. "Hunter and I have been seeing each other for seven months now," she said in her confident way. You'd have to know her really well to see the anxiety in her eyes. "We did the getting-to-know-you thing, and then we found we were getting serious about each other. The sex is good, but who knows? Now we're in that period where we're feeling comfortable with each other. But, you know, that's when things come out. I'm getting to see who he really is and he's starting to see more of who I really am. Neither of us is sure we totally like what we see.

"What if he really is wrong for me? I don't feel for Hunter what I felt for Frank. Sometimes Hunter gets so wrapped up in work—he gets his work head on and suddenly it's like I don't exist. That's very scary for me.

"I'm seeing other things about Hunter that aren't great. I get glimpses that tell me maybe he's not as much fun as I thought he was. And this jealous side of him is coming out. So, you know, I have my doubts. If you ask me I'll say, no, I don't completely trust him. Then part of me starts to weaken—I think, what the hell, why not just go with this. But I can't do that because I don't trust myself to see the truth. I'm not even sure that if I saw the truth I'd be able to act on it.

"I don't want to feel this way. I'm just so worried that my old patterns are going to kick in where I hang in there and hang in there, like it's my ego wanting to make the relationship work. I know I never want to get hurt again the way I got hurt with Frank."

So what was Tracy's problem with Hunter? Or was there no problem with him because the real problem was unfinished business with Frank?

Answer? The real problem was the unfinished business. Tracy was simply not ready for a new relationship. She was lonely, mostly because she missed Frank. She was mad at Frank, which made it feel a lot like wanting to move on. And in reality Frank was still out there, still single, and their relationship had never really ended. It had been wonderful except for his moving to New York.

No wonder Tracy had trouble reading the chemistry she had with Hunter. I talked with Tracy for hours about these relationships. When she described their good times, I saw how much was there. And there was less friction than there is for most couples. The stuff about Hunter getting so tied up with work? He didn't work any longer hours than Frank had. Jealous and no fun? When I asked for evidence, Tracy's examples were embarrassingly thin.

It's hard to carry a torch for two guys at the same time. Tracy was still carrying a torch for Frank. Before she'd be in a position to see the chemistry she had with Hunter, she'd have to extinguish her torch for Frank. She wasn't ready to do either.

There are so many ways not being ready takes its toll. The worst, I think, is that you're liable to make huge mistakes reading your chemistry. You can be so gun-shy that you run away from a guy even though things are really good with him. You can be so needy that you jump into some guy's arms even though he's a horror show. It also changes the way you behave in a relationship. Getting hyperaggressive just so you can take care of yourself, not because of anything your guy did but because of the stuff your ex did. Being too clingy. Too distant. Too weird, from your guy's point of view. All because you're not ready.

THE GUY SPEAKS: *"Yeah, if there's one thing I wish women would get straight, please, please, don't start up a relationship with me until you're ready to be in a relationship, okay? Okay, some guy screwed you over. Okay, you're really sad about some guy dumping you. But deal with it first, go into therapy, whatever. So that when you*

> *and I get together I won't have to deal with your shit from your ex."*

THE SIGNS THAT SHOW YOU'RE NOT READY

Tracy shows how deeply things can get screwed up when you're in a relationship you're not ready for. *Are you afraid that's what's going on now for you?* It might help if you understood that there are many reasons why you might not be ready for your new relationship. Let's go through these reasons one at a time. Check off any that apply to you. If none apply, then you know you're ready.

You're still carrying a torch for an ex

It's not about whether the relationship is over. It's about whether you're over the relationship. I worked with a woman whose boyfriend had died five years earlier. She felt so guilty about the games she'd played with him, even though she'd been convinced that she'd finally found the perfect guy, that even years later she was still obsessed with him. It's easy to say that she shouldn't have been obsessed. And she sure needed help. But the torch she was carrying was a reality.

Has your torch been extinguished?

You're over your ex if you're no longer flooded with charged thoughts and feelings about him.

Sure, you still might have thoughts about him. Most of us have thoughts about most of our exes from time to time. They're how we think about our life. But are you flooded with these thoughts? Do thoughts of your ex surge through your mind and heart, sweeping everything before them?

And are these thoughts charged? Do you feel love or hatred or regret or yearning or terrible sadness when you have these thoughts?

No flooding, no charge? No problem. But if you're still flooded with charged thoughts and feelings, then you're not over him yet.

Based on these criteria, are you over your ex?

Yes _____ No _____

If you have to admit that you're not over him, don't despair. You can get over him. And if you want to, you will.

Maybe you need more time. Maybe you need some casual relationships, with guys you know you'd never marry, a kind of man-sorbet to cleanse your palate. Maybe you need to talk to a friend or a therapist about the torch you're carrying for your ex.

But here's what you don't need. You don't need a serious relationship to clear away the old one. It doesn't work like that. You simply can't read the chemistry in a new relationship until you clear away the old one. And you'll just end up carrying the torch all the more.

When you stop being flooded with charged thoughts and feelings about your ex, that's one sign that you're ready for a new relationship.

Until then, what do you do about your guy? Well, since you're not over your ex, you really can't tell what kind of chemistry you have with him, so you're flying blind. If deep down you're pretty sure that he's an amazing, terrific guy, why break up with him? Hang in there until you finally put your ex behind you. Then you'll be able to see what your chemistry with him really is. But whatever you do, don't make a commitment to him until you've gotten over your ex.

***You haven't had enough experience to recognize
the kind of person you want to be with***

If you've just come out of a long relationship or if you don't
have much experience with men, then how can you say that
you know what you want? You're like someone who's never
eaten ice cream. Once you try your first flavor, it's probably
going to be so exciting initially that you're not going to want to
think about other flavors. But until you've tried a lot of different
flavors, how do you know that the first one you tried won't turn
out to be the flavor you like least?

Neil got dumped by a woman even though things were going
great in their relationship. Why did Suli dump him? Because
things were so good, she was convinced that things could be
good with many guys—she'd only been with one guy before
Neil and it had been a disaster. So she thought about her lack of
experience and realized she wanted to check out as many different kinds of guys as possible. This was sad for Neil, but Suli did
the right thing. Without experience, how could she know that
Neil stacked up well against the competition?

The question you need to ask yourself is: "Have I had enough
experience to show me what works for me and what doesn't
when it comes to guys?" For example, you might've been with a
feisty, hardworking type before and thought that now it would be
great if only you could be with a more relaxed guy who wasn't
so consumed by ambition. But you might need to check out
what being with a relaxed guy is really like. You might be bored
out of your skull. Maybe the feisty, hardworking type is a challenge, but maybe you need the challenge.

Or maybe you're tired of practical guys and think it would be
great to be with an artist of some sort. But maybe you'd find
that artists are just as practical in their own way—they're just
practical without much money to show for it. Maybe that's not
a good deal for you!

You're ready for a new relationship only if *based on experience* you know the kind of guy who's right for you.

Do you know what kind of guy is right for you?
Yes _____ No _____

So suppose you haven't had enough experience to get a clear sense of who's right for you. What do you do? Break up with your guy even though your chemistry is terrific? This is one of the toughest calls you can make. There you are inside yourself feeling that he's right for you. The fit feels good. And here I come along saying, yeah, but have you had enough experience to know how you really feel? Here's the only way I know how to bottom line this.

If you've had only a little experience, be very, very careful. If all your friends are telling you that you can do much better, maybe they're right. If you smell a rat in spite of the fact that he seems to come out well in the chemistry department, maybe you're right. And if the chemistry's borderline, then don't cheat yourself— you can do a lot better. Put him on hold if you can and try to have just enough adventures in the land of love to quell any lingering doubts about who's right for you.

You're still angry at your ex

"I'm so over Doug," Lacey, 37, said. Doug was her abusive ex-husband. He never beat her, but he shoved her, threatened her, yelled a lot, and put her down all the time. She finally dumped him when she became afraid he would hurt their five-year-old son. These days she has little to do with him.

But she only thought she was over Doug. Two years after their divorce was finalized, she met Will, someone she described as a "very nice" man. His calm, comfortable manner made her feel safe. The safer she felt, the more she got in touch with her feelings. And that's when she realized that Doug, like a giant planet, still exerted enormous gravitational pull over her emotions. So she found she couldn't help talking about Doug to Will. Soon "Doug talk" was taking over. She told Will he was great, because he was so different from Doug. The safer she felt with Will, the more she poured out her heart about what she'd had to put up with with Doug.

Not surprisingly, Will started wondering what kind of ex-obsessed woman he was dealing with. When he finally complained about all the "Doug talk," Lacey was shocked and accused him of being unsupportive. "That's the kind of thing Doug would say," Lacey said. Finally Will dumped Lacey because he was sick of Doug.

You're still angry with your ex if you answer yes to the following two questions:

Do you find that you're frequently filled with anger toward your ex that seems to come out of nowhere?
Yes _____ No _____

If yes, that's a bad sign. You see, it's not a problem if you still feel anger when you *force* yourself to think about your ex. That's like there's a drawer where your anger sits and, sure, when you open the drawer, your anger's there. The problem comes when your anger keeps climbing out of the drawer and running around whenever it wants.

Does anger at your ex play a role in your relationship with your
   new guy?
Yes _____ No _____

Yes is a bad sign here, too. It's not a problem if you happen to talk about your ex every now and then and when you do your angry feelings come up. But you saw what happened for Lacey. In situations like that it's almost as if your anger at your ex takes over and becomes more important to you than your feelings for your new guy.

You have to be honest with yourself. You may deny that you're "walking around angry" at your ex. But if your new guy does something that remotely reminds you of your ex and you blow up at him for that (like Lacey getting mad because she felt Will was abusive when all he said was that he was sick of all the "Doug talk"), you're still angry at your ex. And it doesn't do any good for you to say that you "shouldn't" be carrying that anger around. If you are, you are, and that's that.

The reason you're not ready for a new relationship if you're still angry with your ex is that this is yet one more way for you to misread the chemistry. Imagine if you wanted to know what someone looked like but you held a giant distorting lens in front of his or her face. How would you ever know the truth?

When it comes to reading the chemistry, you might think you're safe because he doesn't make you feel unsafe the way your ex did. Well, whoop-de-do. But isn't this preventing you from being aware of other ways he might be making you feel unsafe? Your ex was a liar, let's say, so you put your guy under the microscope to see if he's lying. But this prevents you from noticing that he's a very closed-off guy. He never lies, but he never talks much, either. What good does that do you?

Worst of all, perhaps, being angry at your ex might cause you to take a pass on a truly terrific guy. Let's say your ex cheated on you. That's enough to make any woman angry for a long time. So now along comes your guy and, uh-oh, he works with women, and he's even good friends with women. Every time he tells you an innocent story about one of them, you get mad. But what did he do? The fact that he's comfortable with women might help him understand *you* better. He could be the catch of the century and you just wouldn't see it through your anger at your ex.

So what do you do if you're still angry with your ex? First, acknowledge that fact. Second, put your current relationship on hold. Whatever stage you're at, just stay there until you can put your anger behind you.

That brings up the third thing you should do. Deal with your anger. Don't just sit around waiting for it to lift, like fog. What you need to do is talk to someone. Not him, but a good friend, a wise relative, maybe even a therapist. You need someone who can give you permission to have your anger but at the same time give you an opportunity to work it through.

You can't trust that this relationship is right if you thought the last relationship was right, too, and it turned into a disaster

Many of us are afraid that there's something wrong with us that keeps steering us into bad relationships. Like what? Round up the usual suspects. Fear of intimacy. Low self-esteem. Being hung up on Daddy.

Even if your ex was a horrible, stupid choice, there's still probably nothing wrong with you.

You might say, "How can you say that?!? You don't know me. Maybe I'm as screwed up as a loony bin when the shrinks are on strike."

Look, you can think you're screwed up if you want to. It takes you off the hook. "Sorry, can't help it—I'm screwed up."

But here's the truth of my experience. Out of a hundred women who've been through the relationship wringer, only a small percent are so screwed up that they're a danger to themselves when it comes to relationships. When it comes to the vast majority of us, we get involved with the wrong guys not because we're screwed up but because we haven't known what to look for.

Here are the signs that indicate there's something wrong with you when it comes to relationships:

- Bad relationships feel good to you.
- You're not in touch enough with your feelings to clearly see what's going on with you and your guy and to be able to read your chemistry.

Do either of these apply to you?
Yes _____ No _____

If yes, then you're not ready for a new relationship. But most women *are* in touch with their feelings, and for most women bad relationships feel bad.

I wish we weren't so easily convinced that we're neurotic. All this makes me think of Deirdre, 38. She came to me because she had a history of bad luck with men. Sadly, this history started with her father. He was an angry guy who constantly put Deirdre down. All she wanted was for him to love her. And he even made her feel she was stupid for thinking he didn't love her, even though he never did anything to show his love.

So when Deirdre got involved with guys who ended up making her miserable, her clever friends told her she had a fear-of-intimacy problem. According to her friends, she was going with impossible men because she didn't want to get rejected the way she'd been by her father.

A clever theory. Plausible too. But *false*. Here's how I know that.

First, plenty of us who get involved with the wrong guys had great fathers. You can't say that every woman who gets involved with wrong guys has a fear of intimacy, because most of us get involved with Mr. Wrong on our way to finding Mr. Right. Being normal is not a diagnosable disorder.

Second, lots of women with angry, critical fathers find good men to be with relatively quickly. I see it all the time.

Third, check out what happened with Deirdre. She didn't need ten years of psychoanalysis to help her understand why her father made her fear intimacy. I just proceeded under the assumption that she was a normal woman who hadn't known what was important when it came to choosing guys. I helped her understand what she needed to have good chemistry with a guy. I helped her understand all the mistakes she'd made, like getting involved with hot guys who didn't make her feel safe, like getting involved with guys who were good on paper but with whom she had no chemistry, like getting involved with guys just because they liked her, like being afraid to dump duds.

Once she saw the basics—pay attention to chemistry, avoid simple mistakes—Deirdre was in a committed relationship within a year with a great guy who made her happy. What happened to her fear of intimacy? It never existed.

YOU MIGHT BE READY EARLIER
THAN YOU THINK

People often think that the answer to the question "Am I ready to move on to a new relationship?" is always "Not yet." Actually, many people are ready to move on *earlier* than they think. You could be, too.

Sara, 26, had gotten involved with a guy who turned out to be a woman-hating pig. And a morose bore to boot. And she wished she could've booted him out of her life. By the time their relationship was over, she'd *already* moved on. She just wasn't the kind of person to carry around a lot of anger. Her ex was an ass, and that was that. What's more, by the time they'd broken up, she was completely over him. All feelings she'd had for him were dead. She'd mourned. She'd hated. She'd collapsed in fear. But she'd gotten over those feelings the way you get over being furious at bad service at an expensive restaurant.

Sara had something else going for her that makes it possible for a lot of us to be ready for our next relationship sooner than you might think. She was the kind of woman who really liked being in a relationship. It was more fun for her to be with a good guy than to be on her own.

So if you want to be in a new relationship because you like being in relationships, and if you can honestly say that you're over your ex, then don't go by any timetable. If you're ready, you're ready.

Bottom line

If you're having trouble knowing whether to commit to your guy, it may be because he's a borderline dud but it also may be because you're not yet ready for a new relationship.

"Do You Really Have to Like Yourself First?"

I think the first person who made a big deal about the idea that before you can love others you have to be able to love yourself was Erich Fromm in *The Art of Love*. He wrote a long time ago, but boy was he right. Not liking ourselves is a huge way we get into trouble.

We women today have a more complicated relationship with ourselves than at any other time in history. On the one hand, it's *in* to like yourself and be proud of yourself. Watch Oprah. All a woman has to do is proudly declare, "It's taken me a long time, but now I think I'm terrific," and the audience bursts into applause. And in fact, we are more self-confident and self-reliant than we've been for a long time.

On the other hand, too much of this is just on the surface.

We like ourselves when we're pretty sure that we live up to whatever standards are out there. But they're pretty high standards. And pretty confusing, too. We have to be nice but tough. Self-reliant but connected to others. Beautiful but not care too much about beauty. Thin but not anorexic thin. Family oriented but engaged in the world. And on and on it goes.

I see women who talk the talk of liking themselves, but below the surface there's anxiety and self-scrutiny. And if there's someone out there with a story about what's wrong with us, we're all too eager to buy it. We like ourselves for what we might be. But we find it tough to like ourselves for what we really are.

Now here's what this has to do with being able to decide whether or not to commit to your guy.

If you don't like yourself, it's going to be hard for you to trust yourself. And that will make it hard for you to read your chemistry with him.

If you don't like yourself, you're going to be so overwhelmed by your need for him to like you that you won't start thinking about whether you like him until it's too late. And that will make it hard for you to read your chemistry.

If you don't like yourself, you won't want to know yourself, so you won't be able to know and accept what you need. And that will make it hard for you to read your chemistry.

THE GUY SPEAKS: *"It's a huge turn-on for me being with a woman who really feels good about herself. Look, it's such a pain in the ass to be with a woman who has all kinds of insecurities. I can't tell you how often that screws things up. You can't tell her anything; feedback, I mean. You're always having to reassure her. Forget about it. But if she's, like, I'm fine, I don't know, it's just way more likely she'll think I'm fine, too. Things just go better."*

DO YOU LIKE YOURSELF?

So how about it? *Do* you like yourself? I'm just talking about liking yourself, not having a conceited crush on yourself. You don't need to be going around giving yourself shoulder kisses.

It's really hard for some of us to tell. We're too ready to inventory our flaws to be able to glibly say we like ourselves.

I think a huge part of the problem is the way we set our standards. Imagine if one of those people who determine if a restaurant deserves one of those coveted Michelin three-star ratings (the absolute highest) went into your beloved neighborhood eatery. He might well say, "Zees ees zee worst restaurANT I 'ave aivair eaten een." But what do you care? You love it. The food's plenty good enough, and there's plenty of it. You know the people there and you like them. You have fun and it makes you happy.

Why would you judge yourself more harshly than that?

This example might work better for you. Think of your favorite chair. It's comfortable. It suits you. I'll bet it isn't the most special, beautiful, fashionable chair in the world. But you know you like it.

> **That's all I'm talking about when it comes to liking yourself. You like yourself the way you like your favorite chair. You're comfortable with yourself. Who you are, how you look, what you do, the way you do it—it's all okay.**

If you don't like a chair, it's hard for you to look at it. If you don't like yourself, it's hard for you to look at yourself. Is that you?

If you don't like a chair, you're never at peace with it the way it is. If you don't like yourself, you're never at peace with the way you are. Is that you?

Now you should finally be able to determine if you like yourself or not.

> **You like yourself if you're comfortable with yourself and you accept yourself. You may not like your warts, but you like yourself warts and all.**

Now here's a check on this, because it's easy for us to kid ourselves.

You can't say that you like yourself if you don't feel you can show who you really are to your guy. Is that you?

You can't say that you like yourself if you're always working on ways to fix yourself. If, for example, you go to yoga because it helps you relax, fine. If you go to yoga because deep down you think you're a goofball, then you're not liking yourself. Is that you?

You can't say that you like yourself if you have a lot of regrets and shame about things from your recent past or current situation. Is that you?

You can't say that you like yourself if you believe the negative comments your guy or others make about you. (And by the way, if your guy makes lots of negative comments about you, you've got lousy chemistry.) Is that you?

You can't say that you like yourself if you feel there's something important missing in you. One woman was convinced she was sexually blah. "Where's my sense of sexual adventure?" she asked me. Every time she heard her friends or cousins talk about something sexually daring they'd done, she felt badly about herself. Another woman was convinced she kept making mistakes when it came to men. Another "knew" that deep down she wasn't attractive. Is that you?

So how do you stack up? I know. Sigh. Most of us like ourselves about as much as we approve of the way we look in a bathing suit. For most of us, that's not much. So you're not alone.

But what can we do about it?

Liking Yourself Requires an Attitude Adjustment

It's all about getting the right perspective. I drive a Camry. Not an exciting car. Now, if every time I was sitting in my Camry I compared it to a cute little Miata that I sometimes think I should be driving, I wouldn't be liking my Camry very much. Instead, though, what I do is focus on what it is, not on what it isn't. It's comfortable and reliable, and it didn't cost me an arm and a leg. I can like it not because it's the best car in the world, but because it's good enough for me.

Here's another example. Take some of your friends. They may be amazing, but I bet they have lots of flaws, too. Yet you like your friends. Why? Because you searched the world and out of the three billion women on the planet these were the best, the most worthy of being liked? Of course not. It's just that these are the women you've fallen in with, you get along, you do things together, and that's good enough for you.

And that's the key to liking yourself. I like my Camry because it's good enough for me. You like your friends because they're good enough for you.

And you can like yourself when you accept that you're good enough.

You see, most of us go around with a wish list in our heads. "I wish I were . . ." Prettier. Skinnier. Smarter. More popular. More relaxed. More organized. More interesting. You name it. And all this is basically a list of ways someone could be wonderful, and then we compare ourselves to it to our detriment.

What a waste. Let's concede that I'm not superwonderful and you're not superwonderful. And we never need to be. And we know we never need to be because there are people out there—

friends, siblings, maybe even your guy—who know we're not superwonderful and like us anyway. They're not carrying around a list and evaluating us for how we could be prettier, skinnier, et cetera.

If you want to like yourself, dump your wish list. You are what you are. That's plenty good enough for others to like you. There's no reason why that isn't enough for you to like yourself.

Here's what I'd like you to do. Make a list of everything you like about yourself. Big or small. Specific or general. Silly or serious. I want you to write down a list with at least a *hundred* things on it. You may think that's impossible. Well, it isn't. I've done this exercise with people for many years. Once you get rolling, you'll easily come up with a hundred.

It helps to start with really small things, like "I'm a whiz at using Excel," "My scrambled eggs are fluffy," "I have pretty hands." It can also help to look at yourself from different perspectives. What do friends like about you? What have old boyfriends liked about you? People you work with? Children in the neighborhood? What do you like about yourself that no one notices?

Before you know it, you'll have a hundred things.

What you've been doing up to now is focusing on your imperfections. No wonder you haven't liked yourself! All I'm asking you to do now is give equal time to the things you like about yourself. Every minute you spend with thoughts about how there's something wrong with you, spend a minute thinking about the things you like about yourself. If you do this, you won't fall in love with yourself, but you will accept yourself. And that's all you need.

LIKING YOURSELF MAKES ALL THE DIFFERENCE

When you get to the point where you start liking yourself, *reevaluate the chemistry with your guy.* You'll find it's changed.

Maybe because you like yourself you'll realize that the chemistry you have with your guy is counterfeit. You'd thought there was chemistry because it was such a big deal that he liked you, given that you didn't like yourself all that much. Now that you do like yourself, you can see that his liking you was all that he had to offer.

Maybe you'll find your chemistry's suddenly *improved* because you like yourself. Often when we don't like ourselves we put up barriers to prevent other people from getting close and seeing who we think we really are. If you did that with your guy, that could seriously affect the ease and comfort, the fun, the respect, the safety, and even the sexual chemistry in your relationship. Once you like yourself, you find that you can let him in and suddenly it's magic time. However it's changed, this is now a reading of your chemistry that you can trust.

Bottom line

You won't be able to read your chemistry unless you like yourself. Just accept how you're okay the way you are, just be comfortable with yourself, and that's all you need.

"Can I Handle His Baggage?"

"If you want to love me, you've got to love my dog," the guy says. Then you look at his smelly, mangy, snarling mutt and your heart sinks.

Welcome to the wonderful world of baggage. Most guys have it. Some guys have a lot of it. And it can make things really confusing when you're trying to figure out your chemistry with your guy.

But what does "baggage" even mean? It's everything the guy brings into his relationship with you that he expects you to deal with. Big alimony payments to his ex-wife. An underactive dog or an overactive kid. Parents he's committed to helping out with a big check every month. A chronic medical condition. A big pile of debt. A stalker. A crazy mother. The fact that once he punched a boss in the nose, which somehow keeps coming up every time he applies for a job.

You get the point. And now the question of the hour is, What does baggage have to do with chemistry? A lot.

The Chemistry of Baggage

Suppose you had to carry a heavy weight for a long distance. If there were anything wrong with your muscles or joints, carrying that weight would bring it out. And that's what baggage does to chemistry. It's a heavy weight that reveals all the weaknesses in your chemistry. The more weaknesses, the more you've got to beware of baggage.

The problem is that lots of times you fall in love with your guy before you know the full extent of his baggage. So you think, Wow, we've got great chemistry, when, in fact, you just don't know about your chemistry because it hasn't yet passed the baggage test.

You can't assess your chemistry until you load it up with all the baggage.

You have to expand your idea of what baggage is. It's anything the two of you bring to the relationship that's going to be a problem. I know one guy who got involved with a woman who came from a very old, very rich family who'd lost all their money. She was not only endlessly busy with family crises but also consumed by her sense of loss, a huge emotional issue. It's all baggage.

And it's not just his baggage, either. You've got baggage, too. You might've successfully hidden from him the fact that you have six kids until now, but you don't know about your chemistry with him until you see the frozen smile on his face and the sweat on his brow when he finally meets your kids.

How to Handle the Baggage

Here's what women who've been down this road will tell you.

You should get all the baggage out on the table as soon as possible. Let him know about yours. Make it your business to find out about his.

Make sure each of you knows exactly what's involved with the other's baggage. For example, he might say, "I get to see my daughter every other weekend Friday night through Sunday night. Nothing can get in the way of that." Okay, now you know. Also make sure that each of you knows what the other expects given his or her baggage. For example, he might say, "When my daughter's with me, I'd love it if you were around, too. I'd prefer it, in fact. But if you want to make plans to do something with a friend instead, that will be okay, too. And I'll understand."

When it's all out on the table, you'll both know exactly what you're dealing with. It's understandable that you'll want to sugarcoat what's involved with your baggage and turn a blind eye to what's involved with his baggage. But that's a huge mistake.

Of course if you want to play Romance Roulette, you'll hide as much of your baggage as you can and turn a blind eye to his. What the hell? You might just get lucky. Everything will magically be wonderful. But probably not. Probably what will happen is that you'll chew up four years with a guy whose baggage it turns out you can't handle and who can't handle your baggage.

Here's what women who find love do: they get all the baggage out there early so they can see what their real chemistry is. That's your best shot if you want to get full information before you decide whether to commit.

For example, suppose your guy has an ex-wife who has custody of their kids. He might try to hide from you what a horror show he thinks she is. He might have the idea that women aren't attracted to men who complain about their exes. Which is true, of course. Except that you're already attracted to him. Now suppose his ex is a constant source of major, wall-pounding anguish for him. Her hysterical calls at all hours with insane demands, for instance. *That's going to be your life.* Can your chemistry survive it?

There are three main dangers you run into:

1. Not knowing what the baggage is.
2. Thinking you can handle it when you can't.
3. Thinking you can't handle it when you can.

Getting all your baggage out there as early as possible prevents these dangers. Here's an example. Notice how both people have baggage.

Meg, 29, a bright, attractive stockbroker, got involved with Artie, a guy who'd done time twelve years earlier for assault and battery. (His baggage.) It was a bar fight and there were plenty of witnesses who'd testified that Artie hadn't started it. Unfortunately, he'd defended himself in the fight all too well, putting the other guy, whose uncle turned out to be an assistant DA, in the hospital. Rather than copping a plea, Artie argued self-defense and lost. He got nine months' jail time.

Meg's mom's first husband had physically abused her. (Meg's baggage.) So how do you think Meg's mom felt about her daughter getting serious with a guy who'd done time for assault and battery? When two people's baggage collide, you've got Baggage Buildup.

Now here's Meg and Artie's happy ending. They were both very honest from the beginning about their baggage. It's true that their love had to blossom under the withering light of Meg's mom's anti-Artie campaign. Okay, but that was the reality of their lives. The important thing is that they got to find out that their chemistry could stand up to it. By the time Meg's mom finally came around, Meg and Artie had a solid relationship, and a date for the wedding had been set.

If either Artie or Meg had hidden their baggage, it would've been a disaster. As they say in Washington, it's not the crime but the cover-up that gets you.

THE GUY SPEAKS: *"In every relationship there comes a time, like on the third date, when you've got to come clean about the baggage you're bringing to this relationship. Whatever it is. You've got a ton of debt. A bad back. Whatever. Here's all I ask. If I tell you about my baggage, and you don't think you can handle it, how about just not going out with me again? Even better, tell me to my face that you just don't want to deal with it. Here's what not to do: get all involved with me knowing you're not going to be able to handle it, and then after I've fallen in love with you get all teary and tell me you've tried but you just can't deal with my stuff."*

You should give your baggage issues time to work themselves out. Each baggage issue adds at least two months to the time a couple needs to get a true reading on their chemistry.

Sherri, 37, and Sam had a lot of baggage. Let's add up their baggage time. Sam had a difficult ex-wife. That's one piece of baggage. He had a developmentally disabled son who needed special attention. That's another piece. He had an incredibly demanding job at a company in turmoil. That's still another piece. And Sherri had two kids from her previous marriage. That's number four. Plus she was a transplant from the South and didn't know anyone in Boston. Number five. And she was very close to her mom, who came to visit and stayed in their house for weeks at a time. Six.

Six big pieces of baggage. So at two months each that would mean twelve months, a full year, just to get to the point where they could begin to read their chemistry, and that's on top of whatever time feisty, opinionated people like Sherri and Sam would need to sort out their relationship.

So take the time. It's well worth it. Here's what to do.

Beware of fake patience, yours or his. This is where you put up with each other's baggage, but you aren't really dealing with it. In the end, one of you is going to blow up, and you'll blow up big time. If you're finding it really hard to handle his medical problem, or the burden he has with his mom's medical problem, for example, let him know. Don't assume that there's nothing he can do about it. Maybe he can stop complaining to you so much. Maybe he can ask other family members to help out.

And don't assume that because he's so uncomplaining about your three cats that he doesn't mind. Your safety and your future happiness lie in your finding out as soon as possible how he really feels.

Beware of fear. People tend to get very dramatic about how burdened they are by your baggage. But here's a secret I've learned. Most of the time when we freak out about someone else's baggage, it's not about the baggage itself. It's really about our fear. We're afraid it will get worse. We're afraid there's going to be more baggage that we're going to have to deal with that we don't even see right now. We're afraid that our guy just doesn't care about the impact his baggage has on us.

If you could build a telescope out of fear, it would be the most powerful telescope on the planet, because nothing magnifies things like fear. And it's the fear you have to deal with, not the baggage.

So talk about what you're afraid of. Talk about how you need help dealing with your fears. Ask him for concrete suggestions about what he can do to minimize your fears. Make specific offers to him for things you can do to make him less afraid of your baggage. Say, "Look, I really love my cats, but if you can't stand them, then I'll try and find homes for Fluffy and Patches. But Mr. Whiskers has been with me forever and I would never give him away." Good. Now you've got clarity and honesty. If you guys were meant to be, your relationship will survive your baggage.

Bottom line

Baggage is a big deal. It can confuse or even kill your chemistry. Be a good baggage handler by paying attention to your baggage and dealing with it as early and as patiently as possible.

"Can I Trust Myself?"

Jessica, 31, was agonizing over the uncertainty of her developing relationship. "I've been going out with Mike for, I don't know, a couple of months now. See—the fact that I can't say exactly how long we've been going out says something—that there's something missing in our connection.

"We had this amazing first date. Cocktails, dinner, a show, and I thought we really hit it off. Then at the end of that evening he suddenly apologized—he said he was going to be 'really busy' in the next week or so and he didn't know when we'd be able to get together again. I thought he was blowing me off. Fine. I'm a big girl. I can take it.

"Amazing, though. The next day he called. We had a great conversation. He explained some more about his life. He's a consultant. His time isn't his own. I thought, Wow, okay, he really is busy, but he likes me, which is great because Mike is totally hot.

"This has been going on for a while, though—he's available, he's not available. I understand, but the problem is that it's like he has to call all the shots. So I'm thinking, Okay, he likes me, but come on, he's just too busy to have a relationship. But then I start thinking how things are really great whenever we do manage to get together. So is a part-time great relationship really worse than a full-time so-so relationship? And what does it mean when he says that he doesn't have time for me? Interested but busy? Or just not interested?

"I just want to know if we click. Yeah, things are great when we're together, but if it's so hard to be together, isn't that part of it, too? Isn't it bad if you can never get to the place where you can see if you click?

"My gut tells me this is trouble. Either he is one neurotic guy or I'm not Ms. Right for him, just Ms. Right-Now. But when the bell rings, I want to be with him. I'm not sure I trust myself to make that decision."

WHY WE HAVE TROUBLE TRUSTING OURSELVES

If you're in a developing relationship, every time you turn around, self-trust can become an issue. Part of that's because developing relationships are so demanding and confusing. But another part of it is our knowledge of our own history. If you want to send a woman's self-trust level right down to the basement, just show her a picture of her ex. *What deluded, demented state was I in to be with that loser?!*" she'll cry, as do millions of women every day. What they're really saying is, "What the hell is wrong with me?" Whoever ultimately dumped whom, this is a guy who gave her grief, and yet she chose him, hung in there with him, and actually tried to move things forward in their relationship.

And as a result, many of us become with men the way I am with cantaloupes. I've bought too many bad ones, so now I don't trust myself to select them. So I ask the produce guy to do it for me. He thumps, squeezes, and smells each one and he always gets me good ones. This is a man in my life I can trust!

But you need to trust yourself if you're going to be able to figure out if the guy you're with is right for you. It's up to you and no one else.

"How could I have made such a stupid mistake by marrying him?" Lisa, 38, said about her soon-to-be ex-husband. "He's not all that smart, his friends are losers, and he's shorter than I am! We never see eye-to-eye on, well, almost anything, so we're always fighting. And we're both such hotheads our fights get really scary sometimes. I'm concerned for our children growing up seeing it."

How did Lisa get into this pickle? Like many of us, Lisa spent her twenties young and carefree, as if those years were a long, late adolescence. She got involved with guys for fun or on a whim or as an experiment. There'd been the ski bum, the pot-head, the "artist."

Turning thirty hit Lisa hard. She suddenly realized that she couldn't fool around forever. That's when John showed up. He had one huge thing in his favor: he and Lisa came from the same background—both were Irish-Catholic, and both had working-class grandfathers who'd built up successful businesses. Plus John was really sincere. He thought Lisa was the best thing that had ever happened to him. That felt great to Lisa, since she'd never felt most of her exes had cared much for her.

But when he asked her to marry him, Lisa almost said no. They'd had more than their share of fighting and feeling disconnected. There was a voice inside of her, clear as a bell, that said, "*No . . . he's not Mr. Right. You can do much better. All you'll do is make each other miserable.*"

Lisa felt quite clearly the lack of chemistry between them. But she didn't trust herself. John looked so good on paper. She knew marrying him would make her family happy. There was no one else on the horizon. So she said yes.

So when Lisa later accused herself of making "such a stupid mistake," what was she really talking about? A mistake in judgment?

No! Her judgment had been that John wasn't the one, and she'd been right. Her mistake was that she hadn't listened to herself. She should have trusted the voice inside her that said there was no chemistry between them.

You need to know that 95 percent of the time the reason we get into trouble is that we haven't listened to ourselves. If you just listen to how you really feel and what you're saying to yourself deep down, you'll soon discover that you can trust yourself.

Self-trust had been the right option for Lisa and the same is true for you. This is vital if you're going to figure out if you have good chemistry or not. Even if you look back on a bad track record of choosing rotten guys, it's better, and truer, to assume that you didn't listen to yourself than that you can't trust yourself.

This is important because when we don't trust ourselves to know if a guy is right for us, things get real weird real fast.

Sometimes women who don't trust themselves just jump out of their relationship at the slightest sign of trouble. This is stupid because there are always signs of trouble. Always having a finger on the Eject button is a good way to never ever be in a relationship.

Sometimes women who don't trust themselves jump *into* relationships impulsively. As one woman put it, "I don't know what the hell I'm doing so I might as well just go for it." But of course blindly "going for it" is a good way to build up an even worse track record.

And sometimes women who don't trust themselves just don't put their heart on the line at all. Oh sure, they'll be in a "relationship," but they're really standing on the sidelines. They show very little of their real selves. They don't allow themselves to feel very deeply. They're in hiding. And so they wait for the kind of solid-gold proof that's hard to get if you're a woman who doesn't trust herself.

It's scary, not trusting yourself. Especially when you don't trust your ability to see what's real even if it's right in front of your eyes. Let's deal with that right now.

TRUSTING WHAT YOU SEE

Not too many of us actually go around saying, "I can't trust my perceptions." What happens instead is that there's a clue as stark as a bloody handprint in the middle of a white wall, and we just let it fly right past us. We miss the obvious.

A guy doesn't treat us right, let's say. Shouldn't that be as plain as the nose on your face? Hellooo, this guy isn't treating me right. End of discussion, right? No. For many of us it's the beginning of a very, very *long* discussion.

We start slicing and dicing how "right" he's actually treating us. Yeah, he was grumpy and mean the last three nights, but then he was really nice the next night, although maybe that had something to do with the fact that we made love that night. He was really selfish a couple of times, like when he tried to argue us out of ordering dessert because, "They're really expensive here, and you never finish them." But maybe he's just being helpful and practical.

Then we want to know *why* he isn't treating us right. We're sure it must have some deeper meaning. We blame ourselves. What are we doing to cause him to mistreat us? We talk to our friends and get utterly lost in all the possibilities.

Heather, 36, was married to Freddie, the nicest guy in the world. His being so nice made it hard for her to divorce him. But he was *so* boring. Their relationship was dead. The funny thing was that the day before her wedding to Freddie, she'd written in her journal about her fear of being married to such a boring guy. She'd *seen* that there wasn't going to be any juice in this marriage. But everyone liked Freddie. And the plans were set. So she couldn't let herself trust what she'd seen.

After the brief pain of her divorce, Heather continued to struggle with whether she'd made the right decision. It was paradoxical. If she couldn't trust herself to see that Freddie was wrong for her at the beginning, why should she trust herself to see that divorcing him was right for her at the end? This is how self-doubt works. It's a kind of tumor that eats its way into every part of your being until all your insides are riddled with doubt.

The next thing Heather knew, she found herself in a very intense developing relationship with Daniel. As is so often the case, Heather found Daniel refreshing because he was the opposite of Freddie. He was a sexy, passionate, handsome guy twelve years older than Heather. That part was great. Lots of juice. But perhaps because he was older and very well educated, he saw himself as her teacher. He said she was immature and unformed. He gave himself free rein to criticize everything about her, from her fondness for dramatic eye makeup to her superficial, knee-jerk political opinions (at least, that was *his* opinion).

And still Heather had trouble trusting her perceptions. She hadn't learned her lesson with Freddie—that her perceptions were sensible and accurate. Instead, Heather was up to her same old self-doubting tricks, and she missed out on being able to read their chemistry.

Well, she thought, Daniel has good intentions. (Judging a guy by his intentions is a fatal error we make in our developing relationships.)

Well, lots of the things he says are true. (Not seeing disrespectful, controlling behavior for what it is is another fatal error.)

Well, I shouldn't be so sensitive. (Blaming yourself is another fatal error.)

Well, there must be a reason why I've chosen to be with a guy like this—let me figure out what it is. (Analysis paralysis!)

Heather missed the obvious: Daniel was a controlling, domineering, unsatisfied kind of guy, and after she spent time with him Heather almost always felt angry, anxious, and depressed.

This kind of thing is always a bad sign. When you don't trust yourself to see what's right in front of your face, to feel what's right there in your heart, there's a huge risk that there's no chemistry between you and your guy. Something in your head or heart is causing you to make excuses and come up with stories about how he's good enough. Even though he isn't.

How do you know if you're someone who has trouble trusting her perceptions? Ask yourself these questions:

- Do you usually look to your friends to tell you the meaning of what's going on in your relationships?

                    Yes _____ No _____

- Do you find that you often say, "I wish I'd listened to myself"?

                    Yes _____ No _____

- Is the obvious way of understanding what a guy does very unsatisfying to you?

                    Yes _____ No _____

- Do you feel you haven't grasped what's real until you've come up with an elaborate explanation that includes a deep analysis of everyone's motives, especially your own?

                    Yes _____ No _____

If you've answered yes to two of these four questions, then you're at risk of having trouble trusting your perceptions. You're flying blind.

How can you get to the point where you can trust your perceptions about your guy?

Well, what *are* your perceptions of him? They're just what

you see and feel. If you let yourself acknowledge them, your perceptions are something you can trust. They're direct, immediate information, the way you know how hot or cold it is outside when you take your first outdoor breath.

Just the way you have to be careful not to overcook vegetables, you have to be careful not to overanalyze your feelings. Sure, it can be useful to know why he makes you nervous, for example. But you can't ever lose sight of the fact *that* he makes you nervous. And the fact that your guy makes you nervous is infinitely more important than some little theory that would explain it away.

Let's check out what your perceptions actually are.

How does he make you feel? I understand that at different moments you feel various things with him. But what do you feel most often and most intensely both when you're with him and after you've been together, like after he's left your place? For each of the following, force yourself to check one alternative:

Nervous _____ or relaxed _____?
Happy _____ or sad _____?
Angry _____ or content _____?
Bored _____ or alive _____?
Loved _____ or lonely _____?
Like yourself _____ or like someone who's not you _____?

If your most frequent or intense feelings when you're with your guy or afterward are nervousness, sadness, anger, boredom, loneliness, *or* like someone who's not you, that's a bad sign. There's something about the way you and he fit together that doesn't work. But if you generally feel relaxed, happy, content, alive, loved, and that you're being yourself, that's a great sign.

If the signs are bad, don't despair. There may be a problem with your chemistry, but your negative feelings might also come from something you can deal with. Who knows? Maybe a simple conversation about it can clear things up.

Ask yourself what's the one thing he does that makes you feel the way you do. If you can't put your finger on even one thing, then it's probably bad chemistry.

But maybe when you allow yourself to feel your feelings, you will be able to trace them to a single source. That's a good sign. For example, it might turn out, once you think about it, that you walk away annoyed from time you spend with your guy because he keeps taking calls on his cell phone. And maybe if you told him how much that bothered you, he'd stop. Then there's no problem here. Every guy needs to be "housebroken."

It's not a problem if he needs to be housebroken. It's a problem if he won't let you housebreak him. That's why it's really, *really* important to find out ASAP if your guy makes it hard for you to get your needs met. If every little thing is a fight now, what's it going to be like once you get married? You've got to find out, and, by the way, you'll never find out by keeping your needs hidden.

But if your feeling nervous, sad, angry, or bored has been a recurrent theme in your developing relationship, if it grows out of issues that you've tried to deal with but can't make any progress on, then this is a huge bad sign.

What do you see when you're with him? Heather saw that Daniel was critical and controlling. She made excuses for him, but that's what she saw. What about you? Sometimes we get so wrapped up in our ability to overthink things that we lose sight of the other person altogether.

If you're afraid you've done that, here's something you can try. The next two or three times you're with your guy, once you're alone again, write down everything he said or did. Of course you're not going to remember everything literally. But do your best. And this is crucial: be like a reporter, not an interpreter. Just the facts!

It might help to pretend that this is a guy your sister or friend is involved with and that you're spending time with him to give her a report on him.

This exercise can be a huge eye-opener. Here are some of the things women have told me after they've done this:

"I always wondered why I felt lonely when I was with him. I couldn't believe it was real. But when I kept track of our conversations, I couldn't escape it. Every time I said something, like how I was feeling or what I'd been doing, he changed the subject. No wonder I feel lonely. I don't know why he's doing that. But I can't deny that that's what he's doing."

And once you stop making excuses for your guy, you'll see that what he does is who he is. And you've seen it all along.

"I was so glad I did this exercise. I'd known that I'd felt uncomfortable too much of the time with Larry, but I kind of denied it because Larry had this easygoing, friendly manner, like butter wouldn't melt in his mouth or whatever the expression is. But when I kept track, I saw that he kept giving me these little digs and putdowns and criticisms. Like once I knocked over an open box of cereal and Larry said, 'That's so like you.' He didn't sound angry. It's just that all his comments were like that. It was like he was always holding up a mirror to me and in that mirror I was always a mess. No wonder I felt uncomfortable with him. Larry either didn't like me or didn't respect me. An idiot could see it."

If you pay attention to how you feel and what you see, you'll realize that your perceptions are accurate and you can trust them, and therefore you can trust yourself. There was never anything wrong with you. You were like someone who was wearing distorting glasses and blaming herself for being blind.

You don't have to worry about your ability to see what's real. You just have to see what you see.

But trusting your perceptions is just half the job. To really trust yourself, you also have to trust what you do.

TRUSTING WHAT YOU DO

To find love, you have to be able to stay in a developing relationship when it's good, avoid screwing it up when it's good, and get out when it's bad. This involves things you do, actions and choices.

But many of us find ourselves in a situation where we don't trust ourselves when it comes to what we do. This can be fatal to our ability to find Mr. Right. Now here's how to turn this around. You need to understand how you ended up not trusting what you do.

It begins when we're girls. Now, maybe when you were growing up you were allowed to run around and do what you wanted. Whatever you did was okay. Mom and Dad were either very busy or very tolerant. All I can say is, lucky you. That's not the way things work for most girls growing up. It sure wasn't the way things worked for me.

In study after study, and based on my own observations of families and of women talking about what it was like growing up, most of us are given the very strong message that we need to be good girls. To be nice. To keep our legs together. To be neat. To think about other people. To be helpful. To be selfless.

When you check out what's permitted to girls and boys, generally speaking what's considered normal in a boy is considered wild in a girl.

But I had a secret growing up. And I'm willing to bet you had a similar secret. I felt that deep down I was a wild girl. I certainly wanted to be wild. Though I don't think I ever wanted to be a boy, I envied boys their freedom and how wild they could get without anyone really disapproving of them. Even when my brother got yelled at for something he did, there was a subtle message that it was kind of okay, too, because that's how boys were. If I did something even half as bad, my parents responded as if I were evil.

So what do you get when you hide a wild girl inside a good girl's body? You get a prisoner who really wants to break loose. And there's a part of us that *wants* her to break loose.

Out of this truth about women's psychology grows thousands of years of women acting impulsively. You can only rein in the wild girl so long before she busts loose. And you and I can point to times in our lives when the wild girl broke out and let it rip.

And whenever we do this, there's a part of us that's rooting for this to happen. "Good for me," we say. Every impulsive act is like a line in our own emancipation proclamation.

The problem with this, if we're honest with ourselves, is that the wild girl inside us is *wild*. No one's going to have a sudden wild impulse to walk around the house dusting the knickknacks. No. Here's what we *do* do. We're with a guy and he's getting on our nerves. Not intentionally. But he's just being uncommunicative or stubborn or something. The next thing you know we snap. We yell. We make a scene. We walk out. We break up with him.

And we feel good while we're doing it, because we've set the wild girl free.

Afterward, though, regrets set in. We can't believe what we've done. We want him to understand and forgive. Hey, man, it just came out. I didn't mean it.

But guys don't have wild girls, or rather wild boys, trapped inside them that they're rooting for. So they think of our impulses as choices. They don't understand. They take it all way too seriously. They get really hurt or really angry.

You take this little dynamic and play it out over nine, fifteen years of a woman's relationship history, starting in high school, and you can get a woman who has seriously lost her ability to trust what she does. She may still root for the wild girl in her, but that wild girl is now a big problem to her, as is her ability to control that wild girl.

And that's one of the most important ways we start not being able to trust ourselves.

Now what happens to us when this pattern keeps going on?

Some of us become very careful. We slow down. We try to underreact. We find ourselves putting up with shit much longer than we would've otherwise. But this just sets us up for the dreaded *snapback*. You know how you can take a rubber band and stretch it as far as it can go and then it snaps back hard? Well, trying to underreact is like dealing with this rubber-band thing by trying to get a bigger, stronger rubber band. Yes, you can stretch it farther. But it will snap back harder and more painfully.

So women who don't trust their impulsiveness and deal with it by trying to keep a lid on themselves too often make things worse. Maybe they're quiet longer. But when their impulses break out, they are bigger and more destructive. When you tie down the wild girl, she just gets crazier when you let her out.

Some women deal with their trouble trusting themselves by saying, The hell with it. It's as if they're saying, "If you're damned if you do and damned if you don't, then you might as well *do*. At least it's a lot more fun." So they bust free. Their attitude is, Take me as I am or leave me.

Is this you? If it is, it's a pretty risky way to go in developing relationships. It's true that you need to feel that your guy accepts you for being who you are. And you need to feel the same way about him. But great chemistry doesn't require a perfect fit. It just requires that the fit you have feels good. There will be ways you don't fit together. And then you'll both need to have the spirit of being ready, willing, and able to make some adjustments.

You sometimes see couples with great chemistry still having arguments. But these arguments are okay, because they're working out the ways they don't fit and their good chemistry is the foundation. Then negotiation, compromise, and patience take care of the rest. You know this and I know this.

But dealing with your not trusting yourself by just giving full rein to your impulsiveness is going to lead to your being a very lonely, eccentric person.

So how do you rebuild your self-trust when you haven't trusted what you've done in the past?

> **There's another part of you besides the good girl who takes crap and the wild girl who dishes it out. There's also the wise woman—always alive and well inside you, no matter how frantic and fractured you feel. You need to ask the wise woman inside you what to do. Then listen and do it!**

The wise woman inside you is the part of you that has perspective. The part of you that can see the big picture. The part of you that can ignore the inessentials and focus on what's most important. The part of you that can learn from your experience.

You're probably in touch with the wise woman several times a day, like when you're offering advice to a friend. And who's giving that advice if it's not the wise woman inside you? When you look at it like this, you can see that you can trust yourself to know what to do. You just have to say to yourself, "Wise woman, as one friend to another, what should I do?" You'll find that when you do this, the impulsive, wild girl's words and actions will drop out. The wise woman inside you will offer you much better choices for what to do.

Bottom line

You can trust yourself. You do have good judgment. You just have to let yourself see what you see. You just have to make sure that you really listen to yourself. And you especially have to make sure that you listen to the voice of the wise woman inside you.

Friends, Family, and Other Cheerleaders

One of my friends when I was growing up was named Lucia. She was one of those people who seem to come into your life just so the two of you can have lots of fun together. Sometimes Lucia and I would laugh so hard that we'd pee in our pants, which just made us laugh even more. Lucia had an older sister, Anna, who was very different. Anna was loud, sullen, and bossy, with a mean mouth.

Childhood passed, and at 22 Lucia got married to a boy from our neighborhood. Everyone was happy for Lucia except Anna, who was beside herself. At 26 she was jealous of her younger sister's marriage. So at the wedding Anna threw herself at Lucia's husband's best friend, Vinny. Poor Vinny never knew what hit him. He was snagged.

Anna and Vinny were, as you might guess, desperately unhappy their entire married lives. Vinny never knew the real Anna until the honeymoon, when it was too late. But the tragedy was as much Anna's as it was Vinny's. She sentenced herself to a lifetime of misery, all because she was panicked into action by her younger sister's marriage.

It turns out that most of us are a lot more influenced by family and friends when it comes to the decision to commit than we'd like to admit. For example, you might have noticed among your own circle of friends that once one or two of you gets married, there's a kind of domino effect and more marriages soon follow. Who wants to be the very last among all her friends to get married?

These forces are all the more powerful for being hidden. It's hard for modern, independent, headstrong women to accept that we're influenced by what our friends do. But we are. We just are.

COPING WITH PRESSURE

Family and friends also have a powerful influence on the kind of guy we want to commit to. If all your friends are getting involved with guys with money, then you might feel uncomfortable if you're the only one dating a guy who's broke. If your parents have put a lot of pressure on you to marry a nice, safe, "appropriate" guy, then your desire to rebel might make you reject a great guy just because he'd make your parents ecstatic.

> **It doesn't matter what your friends or family think of him. You just need to make sure that the only thing that's influencing your go/no-go decision is your reading of your chemistry.**

How do you make sure that you've eliminated outside influences? You need to ask yourself two questions:

The first question is: "Who's going to be happy if I commit to him, and who's going to be unhappy?" One of the biggest mistakes you can make is to commit to him just to make someone you care about happy or just to frustrate someone you're angry with.

As you think about whether or not to commit, it's helpful to imagine all the people you know and care about lined up as cheering sections for and against the two alternatives. *"Bobby, Bobby, he's our man. If he can't do it, no one can."* And then *"Down with Bobby, he's a bum. If you choose him, you are dumb!"*

Now ask yourself how much you've been influenced by these cheering sections. If everyone loves him, are you leaning toward making a commitment even though you know deep down that the chemistry is just not there? On the other hand, if there are a lot of people you don't like who don't like him, maybe you're leaning toward making a commitment just so you can poke a stick in their eye.

You might think I'm telling you to ignore all other voices and just listen to your own. Not exactly. For one thing, if you have a very close friend who's known you forever and with whom you're on the same wavelength, she can be enormously helpful as a check on whether your chemistry's for real.

For example, if you've been knocked all askew by the fact that he is so good-looking and sex with him is so good, your friend might point out, "Uh, kiddo, I know he rocks your world because you tell me, like, eight hundred times a day, but do you realize that you're more insecure and off-center in this relationship than in any I can remember? You're not safe with him. You're not comfortable with him. I don't think you think he respects you. You really need to check this out." A friend like this is a true friend.

I've also had lots of people tell me that they didn't realize what awesome chemistry they had with their guy until a friend pointed it out. Why would we need our friends to point this out? It gets back to the way we're all shellshocked and insecure from all the relationships we've been in that haven't worked out. Because we're still virgins of the heart and very wary, we can sometimes be the last to know how great things are.

There's another reason to pay attention to the voices of friends and family. Lots of us don't want to fall in love with a guy just so we can climb into some little bubble of isolation with him. We have a dream of a life filled with friends and family, of get-togethers and barbecues and picnics and dinner parties. If we're honest with ourselves, we know we'll never really be able to have chemistry with someone who doesn't fit into our world like this. It's false chemistry if the feelings you have with him are artificially isolated from your life as you actually want to live it. Make sure that's not the case for you now.

The second question is: "Why am I suddenly wanting or not wanting him now?" Boiiiinnng!—there you are rebounding hard from a bad relationship. The boyfriend from hell. How could you have let yourself be treated so poorly! You feel like taking four showers a day just to get rid of his stank. Then you meet your new guy and he's off the charts when it comes to being a nice, safe, easygoing guy. It feels like heaven.

But maybe it's just *rebound* heaven. Maybe you're just wanting him now because any guy looks good after you've been dating the Antichrist. This is why it's so important for you to ask yourself the "Why now?" question. You want to make sure that you're not swept up by the current events in your life in a way that's blinding you to the real chemistry (or lack of it) you have with him. You don't want to be like my friend Lucia's sister, Anna, and get all hot for a guy just because you're all panicky and jealous. You don't want to be blinded by the rebound effect.

And you also don't want to let what's going on in your life make you pass up buried treasure.

Carole, 27, met the greatest guy in the world right at the time she was starting a big new job and her mother was diagnosed with breast cancer. She had a lot on her plate, and this isn't a great context for launching love. Carole felt she just couldn't handle being with this guy during this period. She pushed him away. They drifted apart.

Fortunately their story has a happy ending. A year later, as things were settling down in Carole's life, she was thinking more and more about how this guy was the one who got away. It turns out that he was thinking the same thing. He called her. They fell into each other's arms and enjoyed the great chemistry they had.

But these stories don't usually have such a happy ending. Once a relationship loses momentum, it's usually hard to build it back up again.

So you need to ask yourself, "What's going on that's important in my life that's throwing me into his arms or driving me out of them?" You need to know before you decide to commit. If you see something going on, like a rebound situation pushing you together or a big distraction pushing you apart, slow things down. Keep the relationship going until you see your life more clearly.

Bottom line

We all wear distorting goggles that can make it hard for us to read the chemistry in our relationships. Lots of times these distorting goggles come from the people and situations in our lives. Make sure you give yourself a chance to end the distortion and see clearly what you've really got with your guy.

ABOUT THE STAGE YOUR RELATIONSHIP IS IN

WHEN YOU FIRST CONNECT

an you tell if the two of you have chemistry on your first meeting? Sometimes. A fix-up you were dreading turns into an evening during which the two of you can't stop talking to each other until dawn, plus you're really into each other physically. Instant chemistry is a really, really good sign. It may not prove you belong together forever—for that, you have to look at your total chemistry after you've fallen in love, after you've started taking each other more for granted—but it sure means that it's worthwhile checking him out more.

If you really click on a first meeting—it's easy, fun, and comfortable, and you feel that good sexual tension— that's all you have to know to continue to the next date.

Sometimes it goes the opposite way. Someone everyone thought was perfect for you—one of those compatibility setups— ends up providing an evening so painfully uncomfortable that you feel time is actually moving backward.

If there's no chemistry at the very beginning, that's *all* you need to know to never go out with this guy again.

But sometimes it's really hard to tell on a first date. Check out what happened to Sandi, 25: "Is there such a thing as first-date phobia? Well, I've got it. The agony of worrying if the guy is going to like you. It sucks. And the whole thing is such a farce anyway. The best first date I ever had turned into the relationship from hell. Of course he was this incredibly good-looking guy that this girl I knew from work built up big time. I was so psyched to get him to like me. I was going to make that happen, no matter what, especially since he had a rep as being picky. Well, I got him to like me, but I wish I hadn't."

READING THE CUES

So what's really going on when it's hard to tell if there's chemistry at the very beginning? Fear is getting in your way. For many of us, first meetings are scary. You're afraid he won't like you. You're afraid you won't like him.

But these fears are not just a kind of normal nervousness. Instead they're a residue from when we were in high school and felt very insecure. Plus it's made worse by all the times that first dates and whole relationships haven't worked out. And these fears put us in the wrong mind-set so we can't read the chemistry. *In fact, the only thing you should be afraid of on a first meeting is that you won't be yourself and so will misread the chemistry.*

When you're afraid you won't like each other, you put your energy into trying to get him to like you and trying to get yourself to like him. I understand. You want to be attractive. You want to be open-minded. But what you're really doing when you're fear driven is depriving yourself of your best opportunity to save wear and tear on your heart.

THE GUY SPEAKS: *"It's taken me so long to learn this. It used to be that when I first met a woman all I cared about was whether I found her physically attractive. I was like, Hey, baby, if you make this cut, you're in. But a lot of those women were disasters. Then I started being more open to women even if I didn't find them all that attractive. But that was going too far. Finally I got it. You really need to pay attention to how she hits you, the whole woman as a package, on the first date. That's the biggest time-saver in the world."*

The snap judgments we make about people are remarkably valid. True, they may not provide some kind of cosmic validation. And people do keep things hidden, good and bad. But your quick takes on people are damned good at showing you how you really feel. If you just have a meal and go for a walk with a guy, you have a chance of learning an awful lot about what he does for you. But you have to clue into yourself. Some women forget to do this. They get so focused on "Does he like me?" that they forget to ask themselves if they like him.

There are a thousand and one physical cues you should pay attention to. For example, can you imagine kissing a guy with lips and teeth like that? He's a little overweight, but does he seem basically strong and healthy or weak and flabby? Those cold, clammy hands, do you want them anywhere near you? Those piercing eyes—sexy, or psychotic?

And there are the interpersonal cues. Does he seem like he's really listening to you, and does he seem like he cares about what you've said? Do you feel there's a connection? Do you feel dominated? Bored? Does the guy give off vibes that he's a weirdo? If he seems like a good package, is it too good to be true?

What we too often do to ourselves is say that, no, no, it's way too soon to make judgments like this. When there are negatives, we all use the same fatal phrase: "I want to give him a chance."

> **You should give him a chance if there's no red light. But that's the point. You only give a chance to guys who pass muster. You don't give a chance to guys who've got a fatal flaw.**

You're going to miss all these cues if you're too wrapped up in wanting him to like you. When you want someone to like you, it's like meeting him wearing a blindfold. You can't see him because you're paying attention to how he sees you. Then you also don't have energy left for thinking about whether you like him.

BEING YOURSELF

And what's the "him" you're talking about anyway? Think about it. How can you see the real him until he sees the real you? And how can you show him the real you if you're so eager for him to like you? You'll only be showing him what you think he'll like. What good is that? Eventually, one day, even if it's twenty years from now, you're going to relax into being who you really are and not who you think the guy wants you to be. Then he's going to go *whoa* and you'll be in the soup.

But we need to trust our hunches. An old college friend of mine told me this story when I got in touch with her recently. She was fixed up with a guy. They met at a nice, quiet downtown bar. He was tall and handsome, dressed like the successful, conservative business type he was. As the minutes went by she had this strong feeling about him: "Strip-club guy." Meaning that he's the kind of basically shallow guy who hangs out at strip clubs. It was sheer intuition. But she didn't listen to herself because, of course, he was good-looking and he seemed so into her. He likes me!, she thought, and all her other thoughts went dead.

Well, guess what. Strip-club guy turned out to be as shallow as she'd intuited. One day she got the flu and needed him to look after her dog. He dumped her.

So what do you do about this? It's not going to work to go and meet some guy for the first time and pretend that you don't care if he likes you or not. You're not going to show up without makeup, without doing your hair, in old clothes. You're going to look good and be your charming self.

What you have to do is play a trick on yourself. Of course you're going to want to see if you have the power to bring him to his knees, to get him to like you and find you attractive. But show as much as you can of the real you, too. That's your real power. Hold on to the part of yourself that says, "I am what I am, and if you don't like me, buddy, that's your loss."

Doing *that* will keep your eyes and ears open. You'll be able to catch your first impression fast and hear your own reaction to it.

GETTING A GOOD, QUICK FIRST READ ON HIM

When we're caught up in hoping the guy is great, we make excuses for him and grade him on an easy curve. We're basically treating some guy we're just meeting the way parents treat their kid who's appearing in a third-grade school play. How do you read your chemistry then? If you're tired of men acting like boys, don't treat them that way.

THE GUY SPEAKS: *"Just once I'd like to go out on a first date with a woman who treated me like a grown-up. Stop trying to impress me. Stop acting fake-bored and supercool. I know you have questions about me. I have questions about you. So why don't you just ask me directly. Yeah, I*

> *want to see your charming fun side, if it's there, but just*
> *talk to me like a person."*

It's best to approach meeting a guy like sipping a wine at a wine tasting. You don't lift the glass to your nose hoping you're going to like it. You're neutral. You're just thinking, Okay, this is an adventure; who knows what I'll find? And whatever I find will be interesting, good or bad. If you approach it that way, if it's bad, you'll know it fast. And if it's good, you'll know that, too.

We often go off to meet a guy thinking, I hope this goes well. Understandable. But "going well" shouldn't be determined by your liking each other. Instead, when you say, "I hope this goes well," it's best to think, I hope things happen on this first meeting that give me as many solid clues as possible about whether I want to go forward with this guy.

Here's a great tip. Go to that first meeting with three things you want to find out about the guy that will help you see if you want to go further with him. The three things you want to find out should be based on whatever you care about, whatever clues you in to who people really are. It's up to you. Then *ask* him about these things. Here are some examples of things that women have told me they feel comfortable bringing up on first meetings:

- *How he spends his free time.* Ask this directly. Be very suspicious of cliché answers like "walking on the beach."
- *How he feels about women.* The fact that he's charming toward you doesn't necessarily mean that he respects women. Guys who have women friends or sisters they're friendly with tend to be guys who actually like women. How to bring this up: ask him to tell you about his friends and then casually ask if he has any women friends. Ask about his sisters.

- *If he likes his job.* How to bring this up: you know you're going to talk about what he does for a living. Ask in a very sympathetic, understanding way, "Do you really like doing that? What exactly about it do you like?"
- *If he has roommates.* How to bring this up: begin by asking what part of town he lives in, then ask him to describe his place, then ask if he lives alone or has a roommate. What you're trying to do is see if he's living in a way that's appropriate for a guy his age.
- *How his previous relationship ended.* How to bring this up: after asking in a joking way if he's single or married, ask him how long he's been single. Then ask what happened to his last relationship—how did it end? And are they still friends? (If they are, that's a good sign.) If you hear about a string of bad women, bad relationships, and bad breakups, that's a bad sign.
- *If he's ready for a relationship.* How to bring this up: get him to open up about his previous relationships. Make it easy for him to talk about the difficulties he had. You can help by talking a little about your difficulties with exes. (But don't go on and on! And no whining!) After he's talked a little about his exes, say sympathetically, "So you probably just want to keep things loose and not get serious at this point in your life." See how strongly he agrees with that. "Of course eventually I'd like to settle down" is guy talk for "If I knew we had real chemistry, I'd marry you tomorrow." "At this point I'm just wanting to get to know different women, to see what's out there" is guy talk for "I'm scared, but if I knew we had real chemistry, I'd marry you the day after tomorrow."

There's almost nothing that's important to you that you can't introduce in a first meeting. And that's one of the most essential parts of your chemistry—when you talk about things that are important to you, do the two of you click?

But what do you do if it's the end of the first date and you're only getting a confusing or murky read on your chemistry?

THE FIRST-DATE TEST

After your first meeting, once you're alone, ask yourself this one question: *If I knew that the rest of my life with this person would be like the last few hours we've spent, would I be interested?* If your answer's no, after you've just spent a couple of hours totally focused on each other and trying to impress each other, you know you don't have chemistry. So that's it. No second date no matter what, no matter how gorgeous or rich he is. You already know he's not right for you.

Of course it may be a mixed bag. There are things you like—"He's so good looking." Things you don't like—"He says his previous relationship has been over for some time, but they still haven't gotten the divorce he says they're trying to make happen." And things you're not so sure about—"He showed up late at the restaurant. He says he's usually never late, but who knows."

So how do you then decide whether to go on a second date with him? It's an important decision. Once you start on a second date, you're moving toward greater intimacy, which means greater involvement, which means getting into something it could take you a long time to get out of.

You can get a big assist in reading the chemistry between you by asking yourself three further experimental questions:

"Would I feel good about going to bed with this guy?" I understand—you're not going to bed with him now. Maybe your policy is not to go to bed with a guy until the seventh date or the seventh month or something. Fine. You're just asking yourself as a hypothetical, *if* you suddenly found yourself going to bed with him, would you feel good about it? Does he seem appetizing to you? Sexy? Trustworthy? Sensitive? Or is there something about him that gives you the creeps? Puts you to sleep? Trust your first answer to the question.

Remember, your first date has ended. He's gone. It's safe to think about whether you'd like to go to bed with him. And you need to think about it, because if your answer's no, where is the sexual dimension of chemistry?

"Would I feel good about introducing him to my friends as my boyfriend?" We'd all like to be with guys who give us enormous bragging rights—gorgeous guys with really interesting, important jobs. But most of the guys we find ourselves on a first date with fall short of this. So, okay, he's not spectacular. But here's the test: If your three best friends suddenly showed up at the restaurant, how would you feel about them sitting down at your table? Does the thought of their meeting him on your first date give you a queasy feeling, or are you surprised at how comfortable you feel at the idea? Would you feel you had to make excuses for him? Or would you be glad your friends caught you with him?

As you know, respect is a key part of overall chemistry. And this is the way you test for respect at this early stage. You're seeing if you respect him by looking at him through the eyes of your friends. If you can't find some respect for him now, when all he's been trying to do is snow you, how will you respect him later, when you've seen all his flaws?

"Would I feel good about going away with him for three days?" Again, I understand that you're not actually at this stage yet. You don't know enough about him. But this is just another hypothetical. Based on the little you do know, does the thought of spending three days with him, just the two of you, scare you or intrigue you? This gets at whether your first reaction to him is that he's boring and obnoxious. Or fun and interesting. And if you say that the thought of going away with *any* guy at this stage is scary, come on, use your imagination. Okay, it is way too early, but is the thought of it less scary with this guy compared to others, or more scary?

This question gets at your sense of how he's going to wear over time and gives you a glimpse of what your overall chemistry might be like.

Now it's simple. You need a clear yes answer to all three questions. If you get even one no, then forget about having a second date. When he calls you to ask you out again (and he will, because you're fabulous), just say, no thanks.

And what reason do you give for flabbergasting the guy by saying no to a second date? "You're a great guy, but I didn't feel there was any chemistry." There's absolutely nothing he can say to this.

Don't make the mistake a lot of us make. We get so caught up in whether the guy's going to call and ask us out again that we forget to check in with how we feel about him. You're calling the shots. And if you don't want him, why should you care if he wants you?

Bottom line

A first date can tell you if it's worth going out on a second date, and for that you need to know your chemistry.

Before You Fall in Love

Saving Your Heart

You're not in much danger of getting hurt until you start falling in love with a guy. The test for whether you've reached this vulnerability point is this: If he were to suddenly break up with you, would your ego be hurt or would your heart be broken? If it's just your ego, you've not started falling in love. If it's your heart, you have. A hurt ego can be very painful, but it's nothing like a broken heart.

This is why falling in love is so scary for so many of us. The bruises our poor little hearts suffer stay with us, and then you can get into a situation like that of Angela, who was 33. "At this point, I'm so afraid of falling in love. It's not that falling in love isn't great. It's *too* great. It's this all-encompassing thing. It just takes you over. I know my judgment is completely shot when I fall in love. It's like this huge sickness that takes you forever to get over. Months go by. Then when you start seeing each other by the light of day, you're so deeply dug into the relationship that it's really hard to have any perspective. I really need a way to protect myself before I fall in love."

This moment, before you fall in love, is your best opportunity to make a go/no-go decision that will save you a lot of time and heartache. That's because this is the stage when we begin to feel that we're putting our heart on the line big time.

One woman said, "A relationship may blossom, but my problem is I usually get freaked out and back out. . . . I don't know why." It's an interesting riddle. Why would a woman freak out and back out when she's starting to get romantically involved? Well, it gets back to the idea of putting your heart on the line. In its early stages, love can feel like a poker game in which you're betting your mortgage money. The stronger your feelings, the more you can get hurt, the more you want to bail out.

You know you're about to fall in love. And you know that contains the word *fall*. And that points to the answer to this riddle. Many of us don't trust ourselves very much when it comes to falling. We've gotten hurt in relationships, but we can't get past the fact that in each case we've said yes to the guy before we got clobbered. Maybe we were enthusiastic. Maybe we just went along for the ride. But we did say yes. When it all blows up enough times, lots of us start thinking we have the relationship equivalent of a black thumb.

But you don't have to freak out, and you don't have to bail out. All you have to do is realize that what you're doing is checking him out. Just say to yourself something like, "Things are really great now. But I've been hurt in the past when things have gotten to this stage. I need to feel safer with him. Let's just go a little slower so we can check each other out more." In other words, so you can check out your chemistry a little more carefully.

It's too bad falling in love is so scary, because most of us also think that starting to fall in love is the best time in a relationship. There's an element of throwing yourselves at each other, and liking it. Suddenly you're spending a lot more time together. You start getting that all-consuming feeling. One woman described this stage as, "Orgasmic All sexual enjoying the person from head to toe." (This is exactly the way she wrote it.) It's like when you swoop down a water slide. No wonder another woman described this experience as "Wheeee!"

This is also a time where we are liable to make a huge mistake.

Love is not the same as chemistry.

Got that? It's really important. We fall in love with guys all the time when the chemistry is actually kind of lousy. How can this be? you ask. I know. It sounds crazy. But there are dozens of reasons why we might get involved with a guy, and once we have feelings for him we ratchet up our hopes to such a pitch that we basically take a flier on the guy and call it love.

The thing about love when there's no chemistry is that (a) it's doomed and (b) it's as hard to get out of as it is for a fly to ice-skate off flypaper. In other words, watch out!

The only one way to protect yourself is to do a chemistry gut check before you fall in love, before you slide into the bear trap of your passion period.

Of course before you can check out the chemistry you have to let yourself have some feelings for the guy. So it's kind of tricky. You are taking a risk with your feelings, no way around that. But you're not taking such a big risk that your emotional future's at stake.

Since you haven't fallen in love yet, all you're really doing so far is checking each other out. You're taking a test drive; you're not buying the car. So take that seriously. It means what it says. You're exploring each other and what it would mean to have a relationship with each other. One woman I interviewed said, "Then something weird happens, like there's got to be something wrong with this guy and you look for it! This is the crucial part; if there is nothing wrong then you are all of a sudden in love." That's the point. Once you've checked each other out and you find it's okay, love can come real fast.

I know it sounds like I'm asking you to walk a fine line, and I guess I am. But what choice do we have? If you put your heart on the line so completely and finally that all caution, all ability to see how things develop over time is lost, then your ability to protect yourself is lost as well. But if you don't put your heart on the line at all, then you'll never be able to read your chemistry—only some emotional vulnerability allows real chemistry to come through. And walking this line is, after all, what women do who end up happiest with their guys.

CLIFF NOTES FOR YOUR CHEMISTRY

Here are some shortcuts for determining your chemistry at this still-early point just before love makes you stupid. Remember, these aren't substitutes for the five dimensions of chemistry. They're just ways to help you see if you have all five dimensions at this before-you-fall-in-love stage. Ask yourself these questions.

Does he get you, and do you get him? We sometimes use other expressions for chemistry. One I like is that the other person "gets" you. He understands what you feel and why you feel that way. You're on the same wavelength. The things you find funny, he finds funny. Your pattern of, let's say, going all out, all day, and then totally collapsing at night makes sense to him. He gets the fact that when you're in a bad mood, you don't want to be talked out of it; you just want to be left alone. He's figured out that you do like to initiate sex sometimes, but your way of doing it is just to be specially affectionate that day. It makes sense to him that it's okay for you to raise your voice when you're mad, but it's very scary for you when he raises his voice.

This is just another way of saying that the two of you fit and the fit feels good.

If you're saying to yourself something like, "He's such a great guy—I wish he got me," he's not a great guy *for you,* you don't have chemistry, and this relationship won't work out for you.

When people get each other, they get each other fast, and you can't teach someone to get you.

Do you feel he's pretty much okay the way he is? I'm talking about things like his personality, attitudes, ways of looking at things, habits, the basic stuff of who he is. Is he dynamic, or is he just an angry son of a bitch? Is he a generous, freewheeling kind of guy, or is he just someone who can't save a nickel? Is he confident, or does he just think you're stupid? Is he assertive, or mean?

You have to sort all this out. That means looking at the guy. Seeing him with utter honesty and total clarity. No bullshit. Then you tell me:

Is there anything about him that makes him not okay the way he is? Are there things about him that are just not acceptable to you? Does he have a fatal flaw? If so, that's a bad sign.

If you don't think he's okay the way he is, whatever chemistry you have is based on an illusion. It means that your chemistry seems good only because you've managed to avoid those areas where his not being okay will destroy your chemistry.

Think about what you'd be setting yourself up for. A lifetime of irritation, frustration, and struggle. You'd be pushing him to change. He'd fight back. You'd get discouraged. You wouldn't feel loved. You'd feel you either have to continue fighting with him to get him to change or fight with yourself to accept what you don't accept about him.

THE GUY SPEAKS: *"My father gave me the best advice. 'A stupid woman will fuck you up.' And I've seen it. It's not about IQ. It's about being someone who doesn't make stupid decisions. When I was in my twenties I was really stupid and this woman I was seeing just dumped me. 'You make bad choices, man,' she said. 'You're going to mess up my life.' I thought that was so cold. But once I thought about it, I remembered what my dad had said, and I realized she was absolutely right."*

Yeah, I know, no one is perfect. You know that he accepts things about you that aren't perfect (at least you hope he does). So why shouldn't you be just as accepting? Well, we should all be accepting. But this is a developing relationship. It's your interviewing him for the job of being Your Guy.

It would be downright self-destructive for you to try to accept something that will in fact torture you and ultimately shake your relationship to pieces. If every woman said to herself, "My guy is who he is, and that's that," very few doomed relationships would make it to the altar. The divorce rate would immediately be cut by two-thirds.

Of course there are flaws and there are flaws. In the end, some are forgettable and some are fatal. What's the difference?

A forgettable flaw is some quirk or problem your guy has that you will be able to get used to. Not that you think or hope you can get used to it. You know you will.

Suppose you discover that he tends to work late. This is a problem for you because you'd like to see more of him in the evening and maybe have him share some of the dinner chores. But as you think about it you realize that his working late means you get home first and have a good hour and a half to unwind by yourself without any added stress. You can get used to his coming home late because it's something you realize works for you. So it's a forgettable flaw.

Suppose your guy has a bit of a potbelly. Uh-oh. Not your dream male body. But fatal flaw? No, you say. (Someone else might say yes.) You quickly realize that for you it's a forgettable flaw. Lots of guys have a bit of a belly on them. Your guy still looks good to you. It's not a factor in your lovemaking. So even though it's a negative, it's one you can legitimately say is forgettable. Because you know you'll be able to forget it.

A fatal flaw is something about your guy that, if you have half a head on your shoulders, you realize will become a bigger and more annoying problem as time goes by. For example, if he's stingy, if parting with a nickel makes blood come out of his ears, if he's endlessly washing and reusing Ziploc bags, and you don't like stingy guys, then you're saying that for you he's *not* okay the way he is.

Being stingy worms its way into every aspect of life. It's not like his being in love with some ratty old T-shirt that he got at his first rock concert and still wears. Stingy is one of those things—like being unambitious, grumpy, impatient, antisocial—that rarely changes in people. So if it's not your cup of tea, it will be your cup of poison.

It's for *you* to say what things about a guy are fatal flaws. Being stingy might not be a fatal flaw for a woman who's stingy herself. Your *Titanic* might be her *Love Boat*. So you've got to know what gives you trouble about this guy. You've got to accept that it's real. And you've got to think about how it will play out over time. Then you've got to be tough. You accept a child who's imperfect. You don't accept a guy you haven't made a commitment to yet if his problems are going to make you miserable and mess you up later.

But if you think your guy is pretty much okay just the way he is, then that's a very good sign. Here's what this means. It means you're going to leave him alone throughout the course of your relationship and not bug him to change. Not because you're suffering in silence but because he really is okay. If you can honestly sign on for that, then consider yourself free to start falling in love.

Does he make good choices? You want to beware of guys who make more than their share of bad choices. I'm talking about guys whose decisions turn out poorly more often than you'd expect by chance. They choose jobs that aren't right for them, cars that break down on them, dogs that make more problems than they're worth, friends who screw them over, you name it. I'll be blunt. If you give your heart to a guy who makes bad choices, your life will be crap.

A guy who makes bad choices will make good chemistry go bad. But a guy who makes good choices can help turn an ordinary life into a wonderful one.

Remember, safety is one of the dimensions of chemistry, but safety is the dimension you learn the full truth about last. That's why it can seem early on that you have great chemistry, but what's going to happen to that great chemistry if you're with a guy who makes bad choices? Don't you think it will destroy your sense of safety?

Anytime one dimension of chemistry is eroded, the other dimensions will erode sooner or later.

Marriage, which is where you want to end up, is not just two people. It's two people plus the life they lead, where they live, what they do for work, how much money they have, who their friends are, the whole schmear. Now suppose you commit to a guy with whom you have good chemistry but who makes bad decisions. Before you know it, money will go, bad things will happen, stress will rise. Either you'll have to be the one who has the whole responsibility for making everything okay, and that will turn you into one resentful, exhausted lady, or he'll just drag you down—you'll end up one of those toothless, tanktop-wearing couples on *Cops*. Sounds good, doesn't it?

But how do you tell if your guy is someone who makes bad decisions? It's not always as easy to see as you might think. You might find yourself with an okay-seeming guy who isn't doing great but isn't doing horribly. And if he's nice and sweet and charming and creative, you might think you've found a winner. But have you?

So here are the telltale signs of a guy who makes more than his share of bad choices:

He seems to have gone from one thing to another a lot in his life, without much to show for it. Lots of people these days change jobs a fair amount. But careers evolve slowly, and people rarely change careers more than once or twice. Don't let the guy sweet-talk you by talking about how he's "a seeker, a voyager, an experimenter," about how he's "still trying to find himself." At best he's a guy who just doesn't know himself or the world. He's a wanderer alright—in circles. He's a guy with a talent for making experiments with his life that fail. If that doesn't add up to bad choices, I don't know what does.

He makes excuses and blames others. As he talks about the ways things didn't work out, the fault is always somewhere else. He presents himself as someone who has way more than his share of bad luck, bad bosses, bad genes, bad parents, and bad friends. But never bad decisions of his own.

Yeah, right. People who make good decisions make their share of mistakes, but taking responsibility for their mistakes helps them become good decision makers.

He talks about how much he's learned or changed but you don't see evidence of it. Some guys try to turn their past history of bad decisions around on you. Yes, lots of bad decisions, but oh! the learning.

Well, I suppose if I met somebody who'd made a bad mistake but learned a huge lesson, and really showed he'd profited from that lesson, I'd be impressed with that guy. But more often than not, people who make more than their share of bad decisions claim they've learned a lot but you just don't see it because it isn't there. Now, they could say, "Well, I just learned the lesson, so it's going to take me a while to show that I've learned it." Okay, but the problem is that you're betting your life on the promise of a guy with a losing track record. In the world of movies, that always pays off, but for real-life single women it rarely does, and you can't afford the gamble.

Who are you? A halfway house for lost souls? Or a woman who wants a chance at love and happiness in her life? If all this leaves you feeling conflicted, here's what I suggest. Commit to the guy who makes good choices. Then in your spare time, volunteer at a halfway house.

So hitch your wagon to a star. If the guy has made bad choices in the past, that's a bad sign, period. But if you can see he's generally made good choices, that's a very good sign, even if those good choices haven't had a big payoff yet. They will. People who make good choices get the big payoffs. And the net result will be that your great chemistry will be protected.

That's important. Great relationship chemistry is like a wonderful lake filled with life deep in the country. It can go on like that forever. But pollution can kill it fast. And the pollution we're talking about here is a life polluted by bad decisions.

Can you see the two of you having a good future together? If your last relationship was crappy or if you've not been in a relationship for a long time, it can feel really good just to get past the early stage. You're so happy to have found Mr. Right-Now that you don't want to think about whether he's really Mr. Right, period. It's like if you've been driving in the country and you're getting hungry but there are no places to eat. Suddenly you see an out-of-the-way restaurant. It doesn't look great. But you're hungry, and it's there, so let's face it, that's where you're going to eat.

But hang on a second. Would you sign on for a lifetime of dinners at that restaurant? It's the same with a guy.

> **If it looks as if you're not going to be able to live the kind of life you want to live with him, there's no point in chewing up the clock with him. There are plenty of other guys out there who would want to share the kind of life you want to live.**

I know too many women who've ended up past the age of forty never having been in a successful long-term relationship because they always went with guys who were short-term good, long-term bad.

How do you check for this? Write down on a piece of paper the three things that are most important to you about your future. Here are some questions to get you started. Do you want kids? Are you ambitious, or do you want a more laid-back but less affluent lifestyle? Do you want to live in the city or the country? West Coast, East Coast, North, South? Lots of adventures or consistency and safety? Put money in the bank or live for today? Follow a certain religion? A neat or a sloppy house? Fit or fat?

You get the point. Just be honest about the three things that are most important to you when you think about your future. And forget all the stuff that's really not so important to you.

Now think about this guy you're with. Can you clearly see him fitting in to your vision of your future? More important, do you have *evidence* for how he'd fit in? For example, you may agree that you both would like to live in the country. But you've lived in the country, maybe when you were growing up. You know you like it. But what if he's always lived in a city? How do you know that his saying he wants to live in the country one day isn't just part of trying to get you to fall in love with him?

> **If the most important things you want in your future are things you know are also important to him, that's a good sign.**

And if you want very different things for your future? Say good-bye to your guy today, cry on your pillow tonight, and start moving on tomorrow—before long you'll find someone with whom you have a chance at real happiness.

> **When a couple clashes over the kind of life they want to live, either their chemistry was built on a lie (one of them was pretending to be someone he or she wasn't) or they hadn't gotten close enough for them to understand their real chemistry.**

And what if you don't know if the two of you can have a good future together? This happens a lot. You haven't been together very long at this stage. And couples who are still just hanging out, making love, going out together, and having fun don't talk a lot about plans for their future lives.

But you have to find out. You could be in for a real shock. For example, before you fall in love is the time to see if you both feel the same way about whether you're going to spend your life on the fast track or not, laying sacrifices on the altar of ambition or just laying back period. You could really be screwed if you waste your time with a guy who doesn't feel the way you do. Obviously, it doesn't matter if one of you is a little more ambitious than the other. But it's huge if for one of you success is everything and for the other success is nothing.

Having children is another area in which you need to be reading off the same page. Since the issue of children is so important, let's zero in on it for a moment. Say you do want kids. Lots of us don't but most do. There are a couple of approaches that work to find out if a guy feels the way you do, according to women I talked to. This is especially important if he has kids of his own.

One is *the putting-your-cards-on-the-table approach*. This is where early on you say something like, "Look, right now our relationship is real casual. That's just how I want it. Who knows how this will turn out. But I know I want to have kids some day. Do you? I'm asking because I don't want to have a relationship with someone where there's not even a possibility of having kids. I just need to know that it makes sense for us to keep going forward."

If your even bringing this up scares him away, I say good riddance to bad rubbish. He's a scaredy-cat. He doesn't understand women—that sometimes we want to have kids, that sometimes we need to take care of ourselves. And he probably doesn't want kids. Hey, you're not waving the wedding bells at him. You just want to know if the two of you would ever make sense as a couple. If he doesn't get this, he's not worthy of you.

If *you're* too much of a scaredy-cat to try this, use *the indirect approach*. Open a conversation with him about the kind of life you want to lead. City or country. Ambitious or relaxed. Things like that. Really get into the details. There's a good chance it will naturally emerge that he wants a family one day. Or he might talk about a lifestyle in which kids clearly have no part. If he paints a picture of how he wants to live that genuinely confuses you about whether he wants kids, that's your opening for casually asking, "How would kids fit into that?"

You can do the same kind of thing for any future-lifestyle issue. Either ask directly or approach it indirectly. But do it, do it now, and make sure you get a clear reading. And the more important an issue is to you, the more important it is to get a very, very clear reading.

Have you put your guy through the basic screening test and has he passed it? What is the basic screening test? you ask. Couldn't be simpler. All you have to do is write down *the top three things that you want in your partner.* Washboard abs? A cool car? Tons of money? A dead mother? A house near the beach? Nice hair? Hopefully, you're looking for things that are less superficial—the three things about a guy that you feel make the biggest difference for your *long-term* happiness in a relationship.

You might think this is easy. You probably had long conversations with friends all the way back in high school in which you talked about things like this. Actually it *is* easy, but you have to know yourself. And you have to be honest about what's most important compared to what's nice but not essential.

One very smart woman I know said she wanted a guy who knew how to have a good time. Nothing wrong with that. The problem is that her search for good-time guys led her to get involved with a lot of guys who weren't as smart and successful as she was. And that bothered her. But she just couldn't accept the fact that she really wanted a guy who was smart and successful. It felt "snobbish" to her. Oh, and she also wanted a guy who was into Buddhism.

She had a lot of relationships that misfired until she put into practice this basic three-item screening test. Then she discovered something that surprised her. Okay, maybe smart, successful guys who were into Buddhism weren't necessarily the most fun guys in the world. But since their being smart, successful, and Buddhist was what was most important to her, she found she was satisfied, and that made fun a lot less important. And while they might not be party guys, they had more fun in them than she would've thought. She was happy, and she found someone who was right for her.

When you use this screening test, you'll know two things. You're not settling. At the same time, you won't be going off on a scavenger hunt for a long list of qualities almost impossible for anyone to satisfy.

And in case you're wondering, yes, you still have to have great chemistry.

Bottom line

That period before you fall in love is your best chance to really check out your guy. It's when you'll save the most heartache and the most time because it's when it's easiest to dump a dud.

GOING GA-GA

Suddenly it hits you, like a migraine or a fender bender. *Boom*. You're pretty sure you're falling in love. This, you think, you hope, is *it*.

Most of the doubts you've had get sucked away and disappear during this stage. It's when you're most likely to want to commit. So what's there to say about this stage when it comes to figuring out if your guy is right for you? Just this: love makes you blind.

If things are great during this stage, you might make the mistake of thinking that you have a great relationship with the perfect guy. Ah, if only that were true. The fact that you're madly in love with someone proves nothing. You know those two and a half million Americans who get divorced every year? Many of them were just as in love with each other as you are.

But still, trust the feeling of love. Trust it's real. Know that it's important. But don't take this feeling at this point as certifying that this is the right relationship for you. Here's what your falling in love does certify: that suddenly, perhaps for good reason, perhaps not, you are very, very hopeful that this guy is Mr. Right.

Falling in love certifies hope, not reality. You can fall in love with a lot of guys before you find one with whom you actually have good chemistry.

But if falling in love doesn't certify much about the reality of your relationship, *not* falling in love means a lot. It's a big warning sign. When I talk to couples who've been married for a long time and who are having problems and wondering if they belong together, the fastest, most solid clue that they'll be happier moving on is that things were never good between them. They never had that wonderful falling-in-love period.

They might have had a going-out-a-lot-together period. But here's what they didn't have: that time where you can't keep your hands off each other. When you feel such a full sense of accepting the other and being accepted. When you find yourselves opening your hearts to each other. When you find yourselves acting silly and goofy like kids. When you miss each other enormously when you're not together. When you share dreams for your future together. When you feel like the luckiest person in the world. When all you need is just the two of you to make a world.

It's very important that you have most of these experiences in your falling-in-love period. Because if you don't have them, there's some important glue missing from your relationship.

And oh yes, one more thing.

You should never, ever make a permanent commitment to each other during the falling-in-love stage.

Oh, you will be tempted. Because it's so *good*. Maybe better than anything you've ever experienced. But the real test is still to come—seeing what your chemistry's like when you enter that post-falling-in-love period.

People who've had disappointments in previous relationships are particularly susceptible to running off and getting married the minute they fall in love. You might say, but wouldn't they be more careful, the more they've been hurt? But hurt also involves loss. And while your hurt makes you careful, your loss makes you incredibly hungry for love.

You can never underestimate your love hunger. It's like food hunger. You could be dieting like a banshee, but if you came home from work starving and found a plateful of cookies on the kitchen table, it's bye-bye, diet.

The thing is that you can satisfy your love hunger without putting yourself in jeopardy. Just be with each other as much as possible during this wonderful period when you're going ga-ga for each other. But don't get married yet. You need to go through the periods where you start being yourself and getting comfortable with each other and when the real problems between you start emerging. It's only then, when you've seen the positives and the negatives, that it makes sense to decide about marriage.

Bottom line

Relationships absolutely need a falling-in-love stage, but it's dangerous to make a permanent commitment to each other during this stage.

SEX

"Sex at the beginning of a relationship is so confusing for me," said Melissa, 29. "I need to know if I click with a guy sexually before I can even think of committing to him. So, just hop into bed with him, right? No, because there's a part of me that's . . . I just feel a little slutty if I sleep with a guy before I have feelings for him. But why let myself have feelings before I know what the sex is going to be like? Yuck, it's so confusing.

"To make things even more complicated, the beginning of my sexual relationship with someone is always a disaster. Don't ask me why. Maybe I'm tense. Maybe I'm too complicated. I don't know. All I know is that before I can tell if I have a good sexual relationship with a guy we need to have had sex a lot. And of course by then I'm really feeling I'm stuck in the glue of a real relationship. I just wish I knew at the beginning how everything was going to turn out."

Melissa's not alone. Sex is one of those topics, like buying a house, that are complicated for most of us. For most of us sexual chemistry is near the top of our list as one of the reasons we get involved with a guy. And as Melissa said, once we get involved, it's hard to get out. There are a number of issues around sex that come up for us in developing relationships. Let's deal with them one at a time.

THERE'S A FIRST TIME FOR EVERYTHING

The question *When do you have sex for the first time with your guy?* is a big one for lots of women.

The women I've talked to are all over the map on this. There are still plenty of us who have the no-ring, no-nookie approach. But there are also plenty of us for whom sex is an integral part of checking out a potential partner. As one woman put it, "Why would I want to go to the trouble of falling in love with a guy I wouldn't want to screw?"

We've got dozens of contradictory ideas rolling around in our heads about when to sleep with a guy. We believe the guy won't buy the cow if he can get the milk for free. We also believe that the guy won't buy the cow if he doesn't get free samples. We don't want to be sluts. We do want to express our normal sexual selves.

The more I've looked into this, the more I've come to the conclusion that every little bit of cow-and-milk-related folklore you can think of around this is true. And so is its opposite. Whatever you do, you could be proved right with one guy, and you could be proved wrong with another.

The biggest mistake we make about when to have sex with a guy is focusing on his needs and not our own needs. Often we'll have sex before we're ready because we feel pressured or because we're afraid of losing the guy. But here's what women do who are happy with their decision about when to have sex. They listen to themselves and focus on what they need. The time is right when it's right for you.

Ask yourself what you need, what will make you feel good about yourself, safe, and happy—that's what you need to know about when to sleep with a guy.

There is one thing you have to be careful about if you do have sex with someone during the getting-to-know-you stage.

It's dangerous to have sex unless you know why you're doing it. And there are a lot of reasons for doing it. Sex is a need, a form of self expression, and a way to get important information about how you feel about the guy, to mention just a few reasons.

So if you go to bed with a guy because you're horny, don't get out of bed thinking you're in love with him.

This is a mistake that many of us have made. It's hard for sex not to mean something for us. That's why many of us still try to convince ourselves that we're in love with a guy after we've had sex with him. We promised ourselves that sex wouldn't change anything. Then we had it and it changed everything.

You're in charge of when the two of you have sex, because, let's face it, if you want to, the guy's going to want to. So before you have sex with him, write down on a piece of paper why you're doing it: "Okay, I'm going to have sex with Bill for the first time. I want to see what it's like with him." Or "It's been a long time and I just want to have sex." Or whatever is true for you. If you do this, you're much less likely to wake up the next day and forget why you did it.

One woman I talked to was Catholic and wanted to marry only someone who was Catholic. Her pattern was that if the guy wasn't Catholic, she'd sleep with him very early in a relationship. She knew it wouldn't go anywhere, so she didn't care. But if the guy was Catholic, she'd make him wait a long time. It was her way of testing how serious he was. This woman had her reasons sorted out.

There's another way to think about making the decision about when to sleep with a guy. It has to do with the kind of person you are. Which of these two statements is *more* true about you?

1. "For me, having sex is a crucial way to learn important information about the guy and about how I feel about him."
2. "For me, making the guy wait for sex is a crucial way for me to learn important information about the guy and about how I feel about him."

Force yourself to answer. One or two. I know both are true on some level. But which is more true for you? That's your answer.

If you learn about a guy by having sex with him—what he's really like, how you really feel about him—then why wait too long? As soon as you want it to happen and it looks like the situation is right for you, go for it.

If you learn about a guy by making him wait for sex, that's fine, too. Trust yourself that this is right for you. Just one thing. If a guy's made to wait too long, he might start asking you what's going on. It may not be that he's pressuring you. He's just confused. So you have to make it clear that not jumping into bed right away *is your policy*. That's very important. You're telling him clearly that this isn't personal to him. He hasn't failed and there's nothing he can do to make you go faster.

THE GUY SPEAKS: *"I think some women think that sex is all a guy cares about. Well, yeah, most guys I know, if there's a good-looking woman, we want to have sex with her. Absolutely. But sometimes we also feel really romantic, if we really care about a woman, and we want to protect her. We also really, really hate a cock tease. So if a woman wants to have sex with me, hey, bring it on. But if she likes me and it's just not her thing to jump into bed with a guy, you know, I can handle it. Just let me know what's going on."*

Whether you like to go for it or hang back a little, don't have sex with a guy until you're able to talk to him about his sexual history and answer his questions about yours. You know what

I'm talking about. Not who did what to whom. I'm talking about STDs, HIV, stuff like that. I'm talking about safe sex.

It's much more than just feeling confident that you can have safe sex with this guy. You need to know that you're with a guy who makes you feel that it's okay for you to take care of yourself. There's nothing more important in deciding if someone's right for you than that.

But eventually you will have sex. Until you do, it will be a huge question mark. Afterward it can be an even bigger question mark. You're going to want to have answers.

The Sex Test

How do you evaluate your sexual chemistry at the beginning of your sexual relationship?

Sexual chemistry is about a real desire for each other—you want to fall into each other's arms the way you want to plunge into a cool lake on a hot day. You like each other's skin. You like each other's smell. You like each other's lips and hands. You like each other's genitals.

I was once talking to a guy who was totally hung up on a woman. "What's so special about her?" I asked. He mentioned a number of things. Then he added, "Her vagina." "Really?" I said. "Oh my God," he said. "Her vagina is in a completely different class from any other woman's." Now *that's* a sign of sexual chemistry. Not horniness. Horniness is wanting whatever you can get. But sexual chemistry in a relationship is desire for *you*.

And sexual chemistry is about an ability to have a real sexual conversation. I don't mean talking about sex necessarily. I mean interacting with each other and learning from each other sexually. There are couples who've been married for decades who are still exploring and experimenting.

> **Sex at the beginning can be great, but when it's accompanied by real sexual openness, growth, and learning, it's even better and is an even stronger sign of good sexual chemistry.**

Finally, sexual chemistry is about what it's like when you actually make love. But how do you determine that?

Sometimes it's easy. If you have mind-blowing sex right off the bat, that answers a *lot* of questions.

But anyone will tell you that it's often not so great at the beginning, often because you still have so much to learn about each other. And in truth, sex usually gets better over time. Okay, then, suppose sex is somewhat south of spectacular at the beginning. Then how do you assess your sexual chemistry?

Remember, chemistry is about the feel of the fit.

> **So the most important question is: Did you feel comfortable and confident in yourself when you made love with him? If so, that's a good sign. It means that there's something about this guy that makes you feel you can be yourself with him sexually.**
>
> **Did you like the way he felt while you were making love, his body, his moves, his sounds, his smell, the expressions on his face? Yes? That's a good sign.**

Did you feel you were on the same sexual wavelength? For example, if you think foreplay is the best part and like it to go on for an hour and he's a wham-bam-thank-you-ma'am kind of guy, you're not on the same wavelength. If you like to experiment and he's Mr. Boredom, you're not on the same wavelength.

If you like him to take a strong lead and sweep you away and he asks you every five seconds what you'd like him to do next, you're not on the same wavelength.

But if you are on the same wavelength, that's a good sign. And that feeling that there is an emotional connection between you is another good sign.

If you guys are having unemotional, mechanical sex now, ask yourself what is it going to be like after you've been together for ten years? And you have to be careful, because superorgasmic, soak-the-sheets, flopping-all-over-the-bed sex can happen without an emotional connection—and you can fail to see this because you're cross-eyed from the good sex.

And it's another good sign if he is attentive and sensitive.

He may still have a lot to learn about you and your body. But so what? How many guys are born knowing just where and how you like to be touched? But if he's a willing and able learner, you've got something good.

Comfort and confidence, attentiveness and intimacy, openness to learning, being on the same wavelength, and an emotional connection are the best indicators of sexual chemistry at the beginning of a relationship.

CAUTION SIGNS

Problems that come up in the bedroom can be real chemistry killers. I'm talking about the kinds of sexual problems that spoil the party. So if there are sexual problems at the beginning of your relationship, don't move forward with it. I'm not saying you should break up at this point, either. Just stay at the level you're at until you see whether the problems can be resolved one way or another.

Maybe the guy orgasms too quickly, faster than most guys in your experience. That could be a bad sign. (This is a good argument for your having some experience. That way if he says, "Hey, most guys only last about a minute," you have something to compare him to.) But it could also be a sign that he hasn't had sex in a long time and you're a tremendous turn-on for him. Once you get used to each other, he might do fine. But you need to see what his pattern is.

Or maybe the guy hasn't set off *your* fireworks, even though you usually have orgasms without much trouble. Here, too, it could be a bad sign or it could be a sign that you need more time together for him to learn how you work. Some women even report that they've cared so much about a guy that it was hard to let go with him at first because they wanted so much for him to like them.

The point is that when problems like these come up in a developing relationship, you just don't know what they mean. You need to give yourself the opportunity to check out whether the problem goes away or stays the same before taking the next step. And if the problem stays, he's got to go. The sexual dimension of your chemistry is just missing.

DANGER SIGNS

What, then, is a really *bad* sign, an immediate indicator that you're never going to have sexual chemistry?

If he seems uninterested in your pleasure or in you as a person, that's a really bad sign.

With a guy like that, it's as if he's unaware of you as a person. He'll make you feel like you're just a giant sex toy, not someone with feelings. You might say, isn't that just the way guys are? *No*. I've heard too many stories from too many women about men who genuinely wanted to be with them and to experience emotional as well as sexual intimacy with them, to think we can let guys off the hook.

So you should have a sense while you're making love that who you are, how you feel, what you need is part of your lover's agenda. Maybe he asks. Maybe he just guesses. But at least he tries. Perfunctorily mumbling "Was it good for you?" afterward while drifting off to sleep just doesn't count.

If he doesn't even try, doesn't even ask you about what gives you pleasure, don't waste your time going further with this relationship. You should say good-bye.

Some of us have trouble seeing the bad chemistry here. Maybe the guy is really cute. Maybe we see his not being interested in us as a person as a challenge: "I'll *get* him interested." Look, we're not talking about getting some guy you meet at a party to ask you out. We're not talking about being on a first date, finding you really like the guy, and getting him to make the first move. No, you two have just slept together. He's just shown you his stuff. So listen to yourself and trust yourself. If he doesn't act like he cares about you at a time like this, he's so selfish or clueless, he's just not worthy of you. You're better off without him.

The good news is that tenderness, a sense of adventure, and interest in you, along with the five dimensions of chemistry, are solid evidence that a life of good sex with your guy awaits you.

Bottom line

Don't think of sex as separate from the rest of your developing relationship. Think of it as a microcosm of your relationship, a way to get a very sharp focus on the feel of your fit.

"HOW FAR WILL WE SLIDE?"

Once you reach the period where you're madly in love with your guy, you're a goner when it comes to deciding whether or not to commit. For a while, anyway. You're in heaven. What's not to like?

But you don't know the whole truth about your chemistry until the excitement of falling in love dies down. That's when you can start to feel your chemistry as a normal couple.

We never know the moment when infatuation has reached its peak. It's just that things are good, great, wonderful, still wonderful, and then one day suddenly not quite as wonderful. Sometimes all that happens is that love takes a dip. You may be more relieved than anything else—your love was too hot not to cool down. But then what? Sometimes infatuation takes a slide and you don't know where the bottom is. Sometimes there's a crash, maybe precipitated by a specific event—the minute you move in together the humdrumness of housekeeping throws a wet blanket over your infatuation.

But so what? It's not a tragedy. You and your guy never expected to live at the white-hot-passion level. It was too all-consuming. You knew it would end, and part of you was glad to get back to a more normal life.

And yet you're scared. You've been here before, in every previous relationship. Love; slide; crash. Love; slide; crash. And that's the question that's got to be obsessing you at this point. *How big will the slide be this time?*

Maybe you'll barely slide at all. That would be great—it's what we're all looking for. It's a sign that your chemistry really works. But you also know you've experienced some pretty steep slides. And what did you say to yourself the last time that happened? I remember what you said. You said, "I don't want to stick around for this ever again." Who would? It feels like a giant water slide where there is no water in the pool at the bottom. Crash indeed.

HOW FAR WILL IT GO?

So once you're just past that peak in your relationship, wouldn't you like to know whether you'll probably stay close to the falling-in-love level or if you'll face a deep, steep slide?

Of course you would. To find out, you just have to answer questions in five areas.

Fighting. All couples have disagreements, even early on. But I'd like you to think about those big, ugly fights, where you both do or say things you regret, where you feel really wretched afterward, where it takes you a long time to recover. The question is, *"Do you find you're mostly free of those big, ugly fights?"*

I'm not talking about spats or flare-ups. Some very happy couples actually have a lot of tiffs. The keys here are the words *ugly* and *big.* You can raise your voices with each other without your fight feeling vicious or dangerous, without it leaving you feeling shaken afterward. But when you have a big, ugly fight, you're saying and hearing things that really hurt or scare you. And it takes you a long time to recover.

> **So would you say that you're mostly free of those big, ugly fights?** *Yes* **is a good sign that you won't be facing a steep slide.** *No* **is a bad sign.**

Nitty-gritty differences. I just want your gut reaction here: *When you think about the little nitty-gritty details of how you live, would you say that the differences between you grate on you?*

I'm talking about whether you need to completely clean up the kitchen right after you eat. Whether you get up early or go to bed late. Whether you like to make love a lot or not so often. Whether one of you shouts and the other can't stand it. Whether one of you thinks it's okay to fart in the house or not. We all have little differences with our guys, but if those differences bug the hell out of you, that really says something about your chemistry. If you have good chemistry, your differences, the kind that exist with all couples, won't bother you so much.

> When you think about the day-to-day issues of how you live, if your differences don't bother you, then that's a good sign. If you feel that your differences grate on you, that's a bad sign.

How easily irritated you are. Some people are basically placid and imperturbable. Nothing much gets to them. Some are easily irritated. Even little things bug them.

Irritability is a huge risk factor for a couple facing the slide. It's like a giant problem amplifier. Just imagine a relationship in which one person is annoying and the other is easily irritated.

Think about how unflappable or easily irritated both you and your guy are. I know you're probably somewhat different from each other. Now add up the irritability quotient of the two of you: *Would you say that as a couple you're basically unflappable?*

> The more unflappable the two of you are, the better a sign it is. If both of you are somewhat irritable or one of you is very irritable, that's a bad sign.

Stress. Some people have much more stressful lives than others. A large part of this will probably be due to a job. This is about more than just the kind of work someone does. It also involves working conditions and whether the boss is a jerk, or an idiot, or (all too rarely!) an angel. But the stress could come from other things. A chronically ill or demanding parent or child, for example. A messy postdivorce situation. Even a very long daily commute.

Here's the question: *Do both of you have normal stress levels in your lives?*

If so, that's a good sign. If one or both of you are dealing with abnormally high stress, that's a bad sign.

Stubbornness. The saving grace for couples under the gun is when both are genuinely flexible and cooperative. Neither needs to have things his or her way or any special way. Both are willing to roll with demands that are suddenly put on them.

But when even one of you is stubborn, every difficulty is magnified. When you want what you want when you want it the way you want it, the fights are bigger and more frequent, little differences get blown out of proportion, stress is magnified, and you're both all the more irritable.

So how about it? *Are both of you relatively flexible people?*

If so, that's a good sign. If one or both of you are stubborn, that's a bad sign.

How many yeses did you come up with? Four or five? Way to go. If you guys started out with good chemistry, you should be riding high for a long time. You probably won't face much of a slide.

One or even zero yeses? Uh-oh. Fasten your seat belt. When

you've got four or five horsemen of the apocalypse riding toward you—susceptibility to ugly fights, being easily irritated, finding your differences grating, having a lot of stress in your life, being stubborn—how could you not be headed for trouble?

But what if you're in the middle, with two or three yeses? Welcome to the rest of us! This is where great chemistry becomes really important. If it feels good to be together, you'll be able to recover from fights faster, and the problems of life that cause big slides won't hit you as hard.

And what about the sexual slide? Can we predict how steep and long that will be? Yes. The better your total chemistry, the less of a slide there will be in your sexual chemistry, even if you start out at a very high level. There are plenty of couples who maintain a good, active sex life even into old age. But it's not about their liking sex. It's about the feel of their fit.

After the Slide

Okay, so you slid. Now it's over, you think, you hope. Now you're comfortable. You have a glimpse of what your relationship might end up looking like.

This is a big moment of decision. And danger. If the slide was scary, you may be tempted to slip into denial. You don't want to even think about things being bad again. But that would be a bad move. This is such a great opportunity to really nail down whether you have good chemistry. Now is the perfect time to go back over all five dimensions of your chemistry.

Ease and closeness?
Safety?
Fun?
Affection and passion?
Respect?

So what's the verdict? Is it all there?

One woman called this postslide stage "irritation coupled with intimacy." Of course, intimacy is what reality strikes when reality strikes. But now intimacy lives in tandem with the truth about who you are as a couple.

Another woman described this stage as "The Mental trying hard to understand the other person and why they don't think exactly like me." There's an important insight here. You'll have noticed in the falling-in-love stage that over and over one of you said, "Oh, me too." You'll have found that you both loved the same TV show when you were kids. Or that you both love some of the same stupid songs that were popular nine years ago. Or that you both really want to get a bulldog one day. Or that you both believe in God but don't think any religion gets it right. Or that you both love day-old Chinese food.

These *me-too* moments are great. And you want to hang on to them.

Don't fail to check back in with your chemistry just because you're busy adjusting to so many real-life issues. Who's going to move to whose city? Are you going to keep his smelly dog that hates you? And get ready for a shocker: *he's* bothered by *your* snoring. But here's the thing about chemistry. Sometimes it's sturdy in the face of reality. Sometimes it wilts. If your chemistry is vulnerable to postslide reality, you need to find that out soon, because it's a bad sign. What will your married life be like if your chemistry is very fragile in the face of the conflicts and confusions that reality brings? That's very important.

The chemistry you had six months ago doesn't matter now. All that matters now is the chemistry you have *now*. And if you have good chemistry at this stage, cherish that fact. It means you have the kind of chemistry that can stand up to life.

CLARIFYING QUESTIONS

If you're still not sure how to sort things out after the slide, here are some questions that will help.

Is he kind? To you, I mean. This is huge. Some guys, when things start getting comfortable, show that they basically don't care about you. Yeah, they want you to be happy, but only because it's hard for *them* if you're not. With a guy like that you get the sense that to him you're just another appliance. Invisible when you work well. An amazing annoyance when things aren't going so well for you.

How can you tell if a guy is kind? Don't look at how he treats his dog or his mother. Hitler was good to his dog, and lots of gangsters are great to their mothers. These are not signs of how he'll treat you. What you do want to look for is whether he has a sense of what it's like to be you and live your life. And that it matters to him that you're happy. And that it matters to him that you're sad. And the reason it matters to him is because he cares about how you feel, not about whether he's inconvenienced.

> **The best sign that your guy is kind is that he's tuned in to what your life is like for you and he's genuinely happy when you're happy and sad when you're sad, and he tries to do something about it. You have to be on the lookout for guys who get mean or distance themselves when you get emotional. That's a very bad sign. It's their way of telling you that when you have needs, you become a huge inconvenience to them.**

What do you think your life is going to be like if you're with a guy who can't stand you unless you have a big smile plastered on your face? Don't be confused by the fact that maybe he's kind when you're happy. That's easy. But if he's kind when you're miserable—without storing up anger—that's a really good sign.

THE GUY SPEAKS: *"I just want a woman to be fair. Lots aren't. One woman told me, 'Look, I'm a woman, I get to be moody. You're a guy, you don't.' The hell with that. I understand, if you're in a bad mood, you want me to be kind. But you have to give me space to be in a bad mood myself sometimes."*

This is particularly important when you're coming off your falling-in-love phase. After all, when you're seeing him start to take you a little for granted, even if you totally understand how normal this is, there's another part of you that's going to feel needy. Remember what an important part of chemistry feeling safe is. How can you say you feel safe if he's not kind when you're needy?

Is he open to other people? There's nothing wrong with a guy who's shy and quiet and likes to spend a lot of time at home. If you're shy and quiet too, then you'll understand. But what if you're a real social butterfly? You like having lots of friends. You like getting to know new people. You like having other couples over. And of course, you like having a social life not just on your own but with your partner. If that's true about you, then here's what you need to think about:

If your guy is a real loner now, he probably won't change, and your social life will suffer.

Most guys are willing to go along with their partner's plans for their social life. But here's the thing. If your guy's a real recluse, or if he only runs with the same three weird guys he's been friends with since the fifth grade—Spider with his dirty long hair and his rock collection (and I don't mean music),

Tommy with his stupid jokes and psycho laugh, and Jake with his crazy girlfriends—then if a social life is very important to you, your life with him will be disappointing.

It's not about the number of barbecues you are invited to. Not being open to new friends is a sign that there's something closed off about your guy. If you're a very social person, you're going to wake up one day and feel stifled.

Notice I didn't say to watch out for a guy who doesn't have many friends. That's not always a bad sign. It could mean that he's just not good at making friends. It could mean that he just has a few old friends. The fact that he's loyal is a very positive sign. And the kind of people his friends are is important, too. Quality guys have quality friends. A guy like this may just need some help. If that's the case, there's no problem.

Bottom line

Some couples go through a long and painful slide. Then they keep hoping they'll get back what they once had. But all the fireworks in the world when you're falling in love won't save you from a steep slide if you don't have good chemistry and if you're vulnerable to a serious deterioration in your relationship. Check out your vulnerability to a steep slide right now. And if the bad signs are there, you should wave a sad but savvy goodbye to your guy.

YOUR FINAL STEP

"What If We Have to Break Up?"

Is It Just the Jitters?

The state of doubt. It can happen as early as the second date. Vera, 26, said, "He's a really nice guy, I think, but, God, he's so intense. And I thought I liked that, but the last time I got involved with a really intense guy, it was like having a relationship with a steamroller. What if I'm making the same mistake again?"

It often happens as you get closer and closer to making a commitment. Sue, 37, said, "One of the reasons I wanted to be with Tony is that we had so much fun. We still have fun, but we keep getting into these big fights that are hard to get over. And they're always about how he complains about his job, and I just can't listen anymore after a while and then he accuses me of not being supportive. They get so bitter, our fights. Is this normal or is this one of those really bad signs?"

Now, doubts can occur at any time, and we've come to expect them. Here's the question that many women wonder about when these doubts come up. Are these j-j-just the j-j-j-jitters, or are these real stop-everything, call-a-time-out, let's-reassess-our-whole-relationship doubts? In other words, when do you ignore them and when do you take them seriously?

Let's get one thing out of the way right now. The mere fact that you have doubts doesn't mean anything. There's no such thing as a relationship so perfect that all doubts are prevented. Lots of times the fact that you're having doubts just comes from all the ways you've been disappointed in the past. There are all the ways you know you can be hurt, plus the vague sense of being vulnerable to an unpleasant surprise. The more problems in your relationship history, the more doubts you'll have.

A lot of this also has to do with your personality. If you're a worrywart, a Chicken Little kind of person in other areas, then you'll be that way about your relationship. So this wouldn't necessarily be a sign that there's a problem with your relationship. It's more about how you deal with things in general.

Here's the real way to tell the difference between normal jitters and well-founded doubts. It's all about your chemistry.

If there's good chemistry, your doubts are just the jitters.

If your relationship doesn't pass the chemistry test, then your doubts are really your way of taking care of yourself. Your doubts are your way of saying to yourself, Hey, pay attention to the fact that there's something wrong with the chemistry here.

And if your doubts are really plaguing you, if you just can't shake the sense that there's something wrong with this relationship, reread this book and reassess your chemistry. Don't let "Oh, it's just the jitters" delude you into thinking things are fine when they're not. If there's no chemistry, you're going to have to do something about it.

FACING FACTS

Cheryl, 28, didn't want to be interviewed for this book. "What do you want to talk to me for?" she said. "I'm in a happy relationship now." I asked her if this was her first relationship. "Oh, no," she said in a world-weary way. "Then we need to talk," I said.

Cheryl ended up telling me one of the best things I'd heard about what you do when you realize that your guy is not your Mr. Right. "I was in this lame, really annoying relationship with this nitpicking guy, Michael. But it was confusing, because sometimes things were really good. Mostly not so good, though. But of course I'm hanging in there, because *that's what I do.*

"Then one day—I'm in sales—I have to drive somewhere and I'm following these directions and I'm noticing there's more and more country, fewer houses. The thing is, I'm supposed to be driving toward a city. The minute I realize that there are fewer and fewer houses instead of more and more, that's it—I pull over and check my map. I find, okay, I'm heading north instead of south or something like that. I make a U-turn and everything's okay.

"Then I start thinking about my relationship and it hits me. It's been really clear to me for a long time that Michael and I have been going in the wrong direction. But what do I do? *I keep going in the same wrong direction.* I wouldn't put up with it for a minute when I'm driving somewhere, but in my relationship I can go on like this forever. I mean, come on. There's something really wrong with this picture.

"That's when I decided I needed to make a U-turn in the direction my love life was going. Michael and I broke up. It was hard, but it was right. In a way, the hardest part was *seeing* that I'd spent two years in a relationship I knew was going in the wrong direction. The next relationship I was in, I swear, the *minute* I saw there wasn't much chemistry, I made a U-turn and got out. Thank God, because a month later I met Mr. Right and things are great. And I never would have met him if I'd stayed stuck in that relationship."

What a great concept. Making a U-turn when you see you're going in the wrong direction. I think that's exactly the right way to think about it.

The minute you see there isn't much chemistry, you can feel confident that this relationship isn't going to make you happy. Make a U-turn.

SAYING BYE-BYE

By this point, you know if your guy's Mr. Right or not. If you're seeing that he's Mr. Wrong, it might feel sad and scary. I understand. But I promise you that in the near future you're going to feel that it's really good news that you found this out sooner rather than later. The sooner you find it out, the sooner you can find someone with whom you've got great chemistry. Just the way the sooner you make a U-turn, the sooner you can get where you want to go.

Why wouldn't you make that U-turn? A lot of times it's fear. He might not be Mr. Right, but he's Mr. Right-Now, a warm body in your bed, someone to go places with, someone to open jars and reach for things on top shelves. And you're going to trade him in for . . . the dating scene?

No. That's the wrong way to think about it. You're trading him in for some terrific guy with whom you've got really good chemistry, and you can find him only by jumping back into the dating scene.

Lots of times we don't make the U-turn because we're afraid of feeling sad. I understand. It sucks to go through a breakup. But this is when we often make a mistake. We think that the sadness we'd feel if we broke up means that breaking up is a mistake. "Well, if it makes me so sad to think about ending things with him, I shouldn't end things with him."

But your sadness doesn't mean that at all. There are two completely different things. One is your recognition that the chemistry just isn't there and so you'll never be happy and so you have to break up. The other is that you're sad because you had a lot of hope and time invested in this guy and this relationship. There's no contradiction between these two things. If there's just no chemistry with this guy, then breaking up could be the smartest decision you'll ever make. And yet you might also need to mourn the good things you're losing.

Just remember that your sadness is temporary. Now you've got the clarity you've been looking for. Now you've got the hope of a much better future.

Lots of times we don't make the U-turn because we don't want to feel we've failed. But you didn't fail. You just realized there wasn't much chemistry. That means it's the relationship that failed. You just hadn't planted the seed of your love and hope and energy in fertile soil. You'd planted it in a rock. That's a mistake, not a failure, and the best thing we can do with our mistakes is acknowledge them as soon as possible and move on.

Lots of times we don't make a U-turn because we're afraid of breaking up. We don't know how to do it, and we're afraid of the pain and mess. Let me make breaking up easier for you.

Breaking Up Is Hard to Do. Or Is It?

It's never fun breaking up with someone, but it doesn't have to be such a horror show, either. We're starting to understand that the main reason why breakups are so agonizing is that people drag them out. That's the key. Never do that. Short and sweet is the way to go.

You already know that you don't want to be in this relationship. So you don't need to have a discussion with him about what you should do. You don't need to get his vote. So the most important thing to do is not to turn a breakup into a negotiation. That's what makes these things harrowing and time consuming—when you give reasons and explanations for why you want to break up. There's no need for any of that.

So here's your breakup line: "I'm sorry, but I want to end this relationship. There's not enough chemistry for me." And that's it. Once you've said that, there's nothing else to say, and you shouldn't say anything else. And if he says that he feels there's tons of chemistry, your line is: "Okay, but there's not enough chemistry *for me*." And, in fact, no matter what he says, your answer is going to be something about how you don't feel there's enough chemistry, how you're just not right for each other, how being together just doesn't feel good to you.

Of course he'll be upset and demand an explanation. "But why? Give me one reason why we can't be great together. We've had such good times together. This just doesn't make any sense."

Now here's where it's so important to understand the difference between a breakup and a negotiation.

The minute you give a reason for why you want to break up—other than there's no chemistry, this just isn't working for me, and so on—the negotiation starts. And that's when the agony starts as well. The best breakups happen when one person refuses to participate in this kind of negotiation.

If you say, "We fought too much," he'll say, "We don't have to fight. I'll stop being so stubborn." If you say, "You're selfish," he'll say, "I'll change." If you say, "Sex was never very good," he'll say, "But you never wanted to try new things." Suddenly, after weeks, months of resisting your requests for change, he's incredibly willing to "work on the relationship."

Every explanation just opens the door for him to get into a big discussion with you that could go on for days about how you don't see things the right way, about how this time he really, really will change, about how it's really your fault, about how everything will be better if you go into couples therapy.

It's possible that he'll hit on some nerve of uncertainty in your decision to break up. And that will drag you back into a relationship you've already seen is not right for you. Don't fall for it.

And don't fall for the idea that this has to be a bad relationship for breaking up to make sense. You're getting out because there just wasn't enough chemistry. It wasn't good enough and it wasn't going to become good enough. You're trying to *prevent* a bad relationship.

AFTER IT'S OVER

There are some things you need to get clear in your own mind before you break up. What do you want your postbreakup relationship to be like? Do you want to stay good friends? Do you never want to see him again? Get clear about this. Then when you break up with him, let him know what you want. He may disagree, but if he does agree, you're that much further ahead.

You also have to get clear about the fact that when it's over, it's over. Even if you stay friends, your romantic relationship is history. So no sleeping together. No rehashing your issues. No trying again—because you know that you can't fix bad chemistry.

You have to be careful. Even if there was terrible chemistry, there was probably one thing about the relationship that was very good. That one little aspect can be the basis for giving you false hope and luring you back in.

And what about your next relationship? The great thing about ending a relationship when you see that there isn't much chemistry is that you minimize the emotional damage and the self-doubt. In almost every case the people who need a long time to recover after a breakup are people who stayed long, long past the time when it should have been clear there was no chemistry. That's when all the crazy anger builds up, along with the sense that you can't trust yourself or guys.

Bottom line

The easier you make it for yourself to get out of a bad-chemistry relationship, the faster you will get into a new relationship. Just make sure you don't get into a negotiation about whether you should break up.

"How Do I Drag Him to the Altar?"

Okay, suppose you've confirmed that your guy's Mr. Right. Great chemistry, great everything. You've checked and double-checked. No doubt about it.

Well, now you have everything you need to know before you commit. *So you can commit.* And if he agrees, you guys are moving forward together. Send me a wedding invitation.

But what if once you're ready to move forward, he starts dragging his feet? Maybe you won't feel so committed after all.

"I know that I'm a pretty terrific person. So why doesn't he pop the question?" Brittany, 36, said. She was echoing a complaint I hear from countless women. "Check it out. I'm an amazing listener. I can really be there to hear what he's saying. And I'm easy to take. I'm a fun person, relaxed, easygoing. I make others feel comfortable. And I bring a good energy to relationships. I'm open and outgoing—I usually do more than my share of the heavy lifting. I'm bubbly and upbeat. If you just give me half a chance I can bring so much good stuff to the relationship. And I'm very honest. I'm someone you can trust. Without being conceited, I'm more than okay looking. *So I don't see why it's so hard for Mickey to decide that he wants to be with me forever.*"

THERE'S NO ONE BETTER THAN YOU

It's truly a mystery of the ages. There's a warm, wonderful woman, beautiful and bright, and she says to some guy, "Hey, you can have a lifetime supply of *me*," and he says, "Hmmm, I need to think about it." Suddenly you've got your guy starring in the role of Hamlet.

It's not as if there's anyone else. All he's got is dread and worry. Some ex of his was a nightmare; maybe you'll be a nightmare. And what if the next woman who comes along makes him sorry he chose you? Not that he can imagine anyone better. But he's just stuck in his dread and worry.

Now what does his having trouble committing to you have to do with your committing to him?

Simply this. You've got your pride. And you don't want to feel flimflammed. So it's perfectly appropriate that you'd be reluctant to commit to some guy that you think might have trouble committing to you. Otherwise, why waste your time? After all, we've all known guys who've kept a woman hanging for years and then suddenly dumped her.

So how do you get your guy to commit?

GETTING YOUR GUY TO POP THE QUESTION

The real reason he's not been able to commit is that the two of you have never had a real discussion about the real issues that are bothering him.

Instead of a real discussion, the conversation goes something like this:

"Don't you want us to get married someday?" she says.

"Look, I really love you," he says. "You're the best. But marriage . . . that's such a big step. I'm just not ready."

"What's there to get ready for? I'm great. You know I'm

great. And come on, we'll have so much fun. How can you not want this?"

"I do want this. It's just that . . ."

What's going on is that it's so obvious to her that he should want to marry her that she can only focus on the reasons for his committing. She's basically trying to sell herself to him. So of course he feels like a jerk saying any of his real reasons for having doubts. After she says, "I'm great," what is he going to do? Say, "Actually, here's why you suck"? Most guys are not that much in love with confrontations to be able to do that.

After beating our heads against a stone wall several times, lots of us move to phase two. "Okay, you're not ready. Fine. Just let me know when you're ready, okay? I'm tired of talking about this. It's too humiliating. But I'll tell you one thing, mister. By the time you're ready to commit, I may be long gone."

But of course the guy doesn't really believe that you're going to bail without ample warning. So all this says to him is great, now he has a long respite from those awful why-won't-you-marry-me talks. So he just stays where he is until you can't take it anymore and go back to telling him why he should marry you.

Sometimes women issue an ultimatum. "Commit by such and such a date, or else." This rarely works, either. I've seen couples easily roll through a dozen such deadlines. All it does is create frustration.

But there is an approach that works. If it doesn't work, you probably shouldn't commit to him, because he's probably far from able to commit to you.

Here's the approach that works. Say to your guy, "You know, maybe there's a reason you're not ready to marry me. Maybe you're picking up on a real problem that I can't see. So do me a favor, please. Make a list of all the reasons you can think of *not* to marry me. I promise I won't have a hissy fit about anything on your list. I just want a chance to go through it with you. If something makes sense, then, hey, there it is. But if it doesn't make sense, I want a chance to knock it off your list. Then we'll see what's left. Maybe once I see your final list, if I were you I wouldn't be ready to marry me, either."

Now, you've got to play this smart. Your future happiness is at stake. So don't make him sorry he told you the truth. If one item on his list is "Because she has small breasts," well, it's not like this is a big surprise. And it doesn't mean that he doesn't find you or your breasts attractive. It may just mean that he'd always thought he'd be with a woman with big boobs. Look, you wanted to know what was on the negative side of his balance sheet and he told you. He's *helping* you. Now you know what you're dealing with.

So after you've shown what a cool, easy-to-talk-to woman you are, go through every item on his list with him as if you were his best friend. Be open and honest.

If one item is "Because I'm afraid you're in it for the financial security," admit that it's a definite plus that he makes a good living. But now you can get him to open up about his fears. Maybe a prenup would make the difference for him but he was afraid to mention it to you. Maybe it would help if you reminded him that every guy you've ever known had money and it's not a big issue for you. It's not why you're glomming on to *him*.

The point is that you're approaching all of this as if the two of you actually were reasonable people. Of course you're probably as scared and irrational as everyone else. But you can at least act reasonable.

So suppose he says, "Because I'm afraid you'll change after we get married." Okay. Honestly, you know situations in which this has happened. He's not insane to be afraid of this. What you can do is point out how he's known you for a long time, how he's seen you in a lot of different contexts, how you're the same with your old friends. This is all anyone could ask for to know that a person is going to be who they seem to be. You could also point out that most of the time when people supposedly change after getting married, most of these "changes" had been visible all along.

And what if it's something like the boob thing? At least you can acknowledge it. "I know you're disappointed. But really, if it's a deal breaker for you, I'd understand. There are ways I'm superficial, too. Just don't string me along. You can either live with it or you can't. Speak now or forever hold your peace."

What you're doing is taking each one of his fears very seriously and helping him deal with it. Some fears, like his fear that you're going to change, you'll show him are groundless.

Other fears are based on things that are all too real, but you can show him that they're far less scary than he might think. For example, he might say that he's afraid of getting married "because I'm so much older than you." So you deal with that. Okay. He's eleven years older than you. But what's the issue here? That he won't be able to perform sexually? Well, there's Viagra, among other things. That you don't have enough in common? But you have tons in common. That he'll die first? Maybe, but that's an awfully long way off.

This is an opportunity for you to offer him genuine reassurance. You might hear something from him like, "So you really don't mind that I'm a lot older? I always thought part of you minded. But now I really believe you when you say that you really don't care."

Suppose he says that you're too moody. You can say, "Yeah, you mean compared to all the other women who are never moody? Get real." But if you're afflicted with nightmarish PMS, you can reassure him that you'll talk to your gynecologist about what you can do about it.

Basically, your responses to his objections to your getting married are going to be one of these doubt-squelching responses:

- "It's true, but I'm not really different from anyone else."
- "It's true, but there are lots of good solutions or ways to work around it. For example . . ."
- "It's true, but so what? No relationship is perfect."
- "It's true, so deal with it."
- "It's just not true, and here's why . . ."

All this gives you a chance to figure out if he's for real. You're giving him the opportunity to either resolve his doubts or put them in perspective. If you do that, then he should budge. This should make it a lot easier for him to let you bring him to the altar.

If not, there are two possibilities. Maybe he's right. Maybe when you look at his reasons for not wanting to marry you, if you're honest with yourself, you have to agree. You wouldn't want to marry you, either. But that's not very likely. The other possibility is that he'll be revealed as the brain-dead foot-dragger that he is. You now see that he has no intention of marrying you, because knocking down his negatives makes no difference. And why should you commit to a guy if he won't commit to you?

But the most likely thing that will happen is that after his negatives have been dealt with, a couple of days later he'll come up to you and say, "Hey, let's get married."

Bottom line

If he's dragging his feet, find out why and deal with the real issues. You'll either discover his true yellow colors or bring him to his knee, offering you a ring.

SAY GOOD-BYE TO MR. MAYBE

Well, that's it. At the beginning there was you and Mr. Maybe. Now you know the truth. You know if it makes sense for you to commit to your guy or if it makes sense for you to move on to someone who can really make you happy.

I've worked hard to bring you the clarity I knew you were hungry for. And you've worked hard to push past your fears and preconceptions to see the truth about your guy. You've discovered how important chemistry is and how to test for all five dimensions of chemistry. You've discovered the secret of women who end up finding love: dump the duds. You've seen a lot of ways to distinguish real chemistry from counterfeit. You've understood why ping-ponging back and forth between relationships with hot and safe guys hasn't worked. You've learned the difference between guys who are keepers and those who are losers. You know the signs that show whether you can trust a guy. You know how to prevent your own issues from blinding you to who's right for you. You're aware of what to pay attention to at every stage of your developing relationship. In fact, you've got *everything* you needed to see whether or not to commit.

Please keep in touch. Visit me at www.MiraKirshenbaum .com. I'd love to hear about how this book has helped you.

ABOUT THE AUTHOR

I guess if you'd never heard of me you'd want to know that I'm the clinical director of the Chestnut Hill Institute in Boston, that I've been a therapist for more than thirty years, and that I do have an international reputation as an award-winning, best-selling authority on relationships. This is my ninth book.

But all that's really just the surface. What's really true "about the author" is that starting from the turbulence of my childhood, I've always cared about love—what it is, what makes it come alive, what makes it work, what makes it last.

You deserve to know that when it comes to love in my own life, I'm picky, and I can be difficult. In a way, it's amazing that I'd find anyone. And yet by some kind of miracle I held out for my own Mr. Right, and guess what? I found him. If I could, anyone can.